International
Hotel English

Other ESP titles of interest include:

BEECH, J.
Thank You for Flying With Us ⋆

BINHAM, P. *et al.*
Hotel English ⋆

BINHAM, P. *et al.*
Restaurant English ⋆

BLAKEY, T.
English for Maritime Studies (second edition) ⋆

BRIEGER, N. and J. COMFORT
Business Contacts ⋆

BRIEGER, N. and J. COMFORT
Business Issues

BRIEGER, N. and J. COMFORT
Early Business Contacts ⋆

BRIEGER, N. and J. COMFORT
Technical Contacts ⋆

BRIEGER, N. and A. CORNISH
Secretarial Contacts ⋆

DAVIES, S. *et al.*
Bilingual Handbooks of Business Correspondence and Communication

KEANE, L.
International Restaurant English ⋆

McGOVERN, J. and J. McGOVERN
Bank on Your English ⋆

McKELLEN, J. and M. SPOONER
New Business Matters ⋆

PALSTRA, R.
Telephone English ⋆

PALSTRA, R.
Telex English

POTE, M. *et al.*
A Case for Business English ⋆

ROBERTSON, F.
Airspeak ⋆

⋆ includes audio cassette(s)

International Hotel English

Communicating with the international traveller

Donald Adamson

ENGLISH LANGUAGE TEACHING

Prentice Hall

New York London Toronto Sydney Tokyo

First published 1989 by
Prentice Hall International (UK) Ltd
66 Wood Lane End, Hemel Hempstead
Hertfordshire, HP2 4RG
A division of
Simon & Schuster International Group

© Prentice Hall International (UK) Ltd, 1989

Printed and bound in Great Britain at the
University Press, Cambridge.

Library of Congress Cataloging-in-Publication Data

Adamson, Donald, 1943–
  International hotel English.

  Bibliography: p.
  Includes index.
  1. English language — Conversation and phrase books (for
restaurant and hotel personnel) 2. English language —
Textbooks for foreign speakers. 3. Restaurant management —
Terminology. 4. Hotel management — Terminology. I. Title.
PE1116.R47A34   1989   428.3'4'024647   88-28796
ISBN 0-13-473042-9

British Library Cataloguing in Publication Data

Adamson, Donald, *1943–*
  International hotel English: Communicating with the
international traveller. — (Prentice Hall English
language teaching).
  1. Spoken English language, — For non-English speaking
hotel personnel
  I. Title
  428.2'4'024647

  ISBN 0-13-473042-9

---

1 2 3 4 5 93 92 91 90 89

Contents

Introduction

The purpose of the course
International Hotel English is a course for those training for or employed in the hotel and tourist business, who need to use English for their studies or jobs. It is also for all non-native English-speaking travellers frequenting international hotels. The areas of hotel work covered are those concerned with reservations, rooms, services and facilities, i.e. those responsibilities involving communication with guests rather than behind the scenes management. The service of food and beverages is covered in the companion course *International Restaurant English*. The emphasis throughout the course is on understanding and responding to an international clientele using English as the main language of communication.

The level of the course
The course is for students who have learned English for two or three years at an earlier stage or who have gained a haphazard and limited knowledge of English while on the job. *International Hotel English* gives them a more systematic job-related English.

The components of the course
This book contains 17 units and a transcript of the recorded material. The accompanying cassettes contain the dialogues and other forms of input for the listening tasks and form an integral part of the course.

The main features of the course
The principal emphasis of the course is on listening and speaking as this is the main area of guest/hotel employee interaction. However, there are also reading and writing tasks which are used for preparation and for sensitizing students to new language as well as for further practice. Throughout the course, attention is given to as much authenticity of text and task as possible.

The course is *topic-based*. Each unit covers a different aspect of hotel operations such as 'room types', 'reservations', 'services', etc. and focuses on the functional language associated with these operations.

Although the course is *not* structural, grammatical patterns are practised when they are useful for expressing a particular function.

The units are *self-contained*. They follow a logical progression, but it is by no means necessary to cover the material in this order. There is a certain amount of deliberate overlap between some units — for example, reporting problems with rooms or giving guidance on hotel services. This reflects the real world of hotels, where situations are seldom totally isolated from each other. It also allows a considerable degree of 'recycling' of material from unit to unit.

The structure of the units
Each unit contains the following sections:

1 *To start you off.* This section has various purposes. It introduces students to the topic and sets off a train of mental associations which will help them to deal with later content. In several units it encourages students to use their own existing knowledge of a topic, since it is upon this that any further learning must build. This section often anticipates vocabulary and patterns used later in the unit.

2 *Developing the topic.* This is the core section of the unit. It extends the topic in a variety of ways. Sometimes the topic is treated in depth, looking at the various ways in which interactions can occur and practising them at length through exercises. At other times the topic is seen as a group of smaller topics which are generally related to each other (for example, giving directions on where to find services, and giving general information about services).

The main landmarks in this section at the listening tasks. There are at least two main listening activities in each unit. The first of these is a bridge between *To start you off* and *Developing the topic*. The second occurs towards the end of the section; it usually contains the new items introduced in the unit and prepares the students for the final spoken or written tasks in the section.

Interspersed with the listening tasks are exercises in guided interaction, vocabulary, matching sections of a text, writing brief texts, etc., depending on the topic under study.

3 *Follow-up.* This section contains more open-ended tasks. Often these involve role-play (guided or partly guided), although tasks involving writing or project work are suggested as well. At the end of this section in many units there is an 'information-gap' exercise. This involves role-play in which one student has access to information which is not available to another student. It also provides an additional challenge, and forces students to use language in ways which reflect real-life situations.

4 *Language reference.* This provides a resource for language use, learning and revision. It sets out the main functions, patterns and vocabulary items in the unit, along with other useful items related to the topic. It is referred to during the unit so that the students can consult it if necessary.

The methodology of the course
The methodology strikes a balance between various current approaches. An important part of the methodology is *communicative* in the sense of offering interactions

with elements of freedom and choice, extending to open-ended role-play with unpredictable outcomes. On the other hand, the material has also been written with *traditional* classroom situations in mind. Many of the exercises are extremely simple in format, involving blank-filling and matching (though these exercises are often quite challenging, and they are never totally mechanical).

Although parts of the material are best suited to work in a class with a teacher, a large part of the material can be tackled by students *working on their own*, checking their comprehension against the tapescript where necessary.

The contexts and situations of the course
The course has been designed to cover a range of hotel types found in many different countries. The settings range from first-class, luxury hotels offering a very full range of services, to relatively humble establishments — though obviously, the emphasis is on the type of hotel that would have a cosmopolitan clientele and staff. The cassette recordings offer many different varieties of English to reflect the sort of language that international hotel employees have to encounter in their work.

Acknowledgements
The author and publisher would like to thank:

Delegates in France
Delegates in Scotland
The Economist
Here's Health
The Observer
Reed Business Publishing

for permission to reproduce advertisements used to illustrate this text, and:

Crest Hotels
The Hilton
Holiday Inn
Marriott Hotels and Resorts
Thomson
West Country Tourist Board

for kindly supplying photographs.

Special thanks to Diana Bruno (Institut de tourisme et d'hôtellerie du Québec, Ministère du Tourisme) for her advice.

Hotel types and hotel activities

To start you off

1 Look at the pictures. What kinds of hotel do they show?

1

2

3

4

2 How could you describe the following types of hotel? Say what you think about each of them in terms of:

— where you might find the hotel
— the owners
— the facilities and services

— the kind of guests who stay in it
— the length of time they stay
— what it costs to stay in it

1

(a) resort hotel
(b) motel
(c) country house hotel

(d) commercial hotel
(e) airport hotel
(f) luxury hotel

(g) congress hotel
(h) guest house

Which of these are shown in the photographs above?

3 Match the following descriptions with the types of hotel mentioned in Exercise 2:

(a) It is built specially to provide a service to motorists.
(b) It provides every facility a wealthy guest might need.
(c) It is situated in a place where tourists like to stay, often near the sea. Guests may stay for a week or two, and usually book in advance.
(d) It provides accommodation for people going to or coming from other countries, usually only staying for one night.
(e) It is often situated in a town centre, and provides accommodation for travelling businessmen, staying only one or two nights.
(f) It provides facilities for large meetings and conferences, with a lecture theatre and exhibition facilities.
(g) It provides low-priced accommodation, usually on a small scale, for holiday visitors or for long-stay guests.
(h) It is situated in pleasant scenery, and provides comfortable but informal accommodation for people who want to relax in a quiet place.

Developing the topic

4 The large motoring organizations *classify* hotels by giving them stars. Thus we have 'five-star hotels', 'two-star hotels', etc. in classes like this:

★★★★★ (5-star) ★★★★ (4-star) ★★★ (3-star) ★★ (2-star) ★ (1-star)

Here are some extracts from the explanations of stars given by the British Automobile Association. Match each extract with one of the classes above.

(a) _____ Hotels with more spacious accommodation, with two thirds of the bedrooms containing a private bathroom/shower with lavatory. Fuller meal facilities are provided.

(b) _____ Hotels offering a high standard of comfort and service with all bedrooms providing a private bathroom/shower with lavatory.

(c) _____ Hotels and inns generally of small scale with good facilities and furnishings; adequate bath and lavatory arrangements.

(d) _____ Hotels offering a higher standard of accommodation; 20 per cent of bedrooms containing a private bathroom or shower with lavatory.

(e) _____ Luxury hotels offering the highest international standards.

5 From the explanations above, find:

in (a) a word meaning *having plenty of room* _____
in (a) a word meaning *a place to stay* _____
in (a) a word meaning *things that are useful to a person* _____
in (a) a word meaning *given* _____
in (b) a word meaning *quantity or amount offered all the time* _____
in (b) a word meaning *attention to customers* _____
in (c) an expression meaning *not very big* _____
in (c) a word meaning *furniture and other things fixed in a room* _____
in (c) a word meaning *good enough* _____
in (e) a word meaning *found in different countries* _____

6 Look at the advertisements below for five hotels. What types of hotel are they for?

WHERE THE GREAT ESCAPE

When the nights draw in and summer is only a fleeting memory, everyone deserves to escape into luxury.

At £145 for any two consecutive nights' dinner, bed and breakfast, The Gleneagles Hotel Winter Warmth breaks are a unique passport to a world untouched by work or worry.

With superb golf and sporting facilities, The Gleneagles Mark Phillips Equestrian Centre and the Country Club, the opportunities to pamper yourself are endless

The sooner you telephone the sooner you can escape.

THE GLENEAGLES HOTEL

For further information contact Gordon Mair, Auchterarder, Perthshire PH3 1NF. Telephone 0764 62231. Telex 76105. Winter Warmth Breaks run from 1 November 1988-30 April 1989 subject to availability.

EXECUTIVE HOTEL

57 Pont Street
Knightsbridge
London SW1X OBD

Tel: 01-581 2424
Fax: 01-589 9456
Telex: 941 3498 EXECUT G

Single: **£49.95** + *VAT*
Double/Twin: **£64.95** + *VAT*
Extra Single: **£19.95** + *VAT*

Elegance, privacy and exceptional value in one of the world's most fashionable neighbourhoods. Buffet style English breakfast included.

PEAK PARK Close Dovedale, 17th C Old Hall. Log fires, 4 posters, baths ensuite, comfort, quiet, fresh home cooking, licensed. Splended scenery, uncrowded walks. DB&B from £22. Brochure: Mrs Moffet, Biggin Hall, Biggin-by-Hartington, Buxton, Derbys. Tel: 029884 451

Brook Linn
COUNTRY HOUSE

Peacefully set in the Trossachs with beautiful mountain views. The ideal centre for touring, walking and visiting the Glasgow Garden Festival. Enjoy our wholefood vegetarian or traditional meals in the comfort of this lovely house. Self-catering cottage also available.
BROCHURE:
Fiona and Derek House,
Brook Linn Country House,
Callander, Perthshire.
Tel: (0877) 30103.

WILLAPARK MANOR HOTEL

Bossiney, Tintagel, Cornwall PL34 0BA
Tel: Camelford (0840) 770782

One of the most beautifully situated hotels in Cornwall

ETB 3 Crowns   Bedroom Category 4

Beautiful character house amidst lovely Cornish scenery in 14 acres of gardens and secluded woodland. Private access to Bossiney Common. Coastal path. Minutes from the beach. 14 Bedroom accommodation, all en suite. TV lounge, cocktail bar, games room. Dinner, Bed & Breakfast £149 per week incl.

Reductions for children. Pets welcome. Open all year.

3

7 Listen to five people who are making enquiries in an information bureau. Which of the hotels above would suit each person, and why? Answer like this:

The .... Hotel would suit the (first) person because ....

8 A hotel may offer many services, including services for people who are not staying in the hotel. For example, it may:

— contain restaurants and bars
— provide a meeting place for clubs and organizations
— offer entertainment and recreation
— stage conferences and exhibitions
— provide facilities for sports and competitions
— provide a place for family or company celebrations

Can you add any other services to this list?
Which services do you think are most important?
Give examples of services you have mentioned, from any hotel you know.

9 Hotel staff often have to talk about times — to say when a tourist group is expected, when a club is due to begin a meeting, etc. Make sure that you know how to talk about times (see Language Reference, page 6).

Georgio Stakis is Assistant Manager of the Rio Hotel. This morning he is talking to Tim Renton, his Front Office Manager. He is telling Tim about the times of various events during the day.

Listen, and fill in the times in Georgio's diary, below.

```
-------  Prince Abdulkadr, Saudi Arabia
-------  Opening, flower exhibition
-------  Wedding party
-------  Lions Club meeting
-------  Seagull Tours
------- - ------  Rio Bridge Club
------- - ------  Brightlights Cabaret
```

10 Now look at Georgio's diary for another day. Complete what he says to Tim, as in the examples given.

```
09.00 - 16.30    Northern  Chess  Competition

09.30            Group  from  Leonidas  Tours

10.45            Meeting, Robert Blye (Servex Hotel Equipment)

11.00-12.30      Lea Social Club (Annual General Meeting)

14.30            make speech (Bell Captain's long-service award)

15.00-16.45      Insurance Conference (delegates check in)

17.00            Opening of Insurance Conference

21.00-0200       Rio Disco Party
```

(a) From .nine o'clock. till half past four we .have.. the Northern Chess competition.
(b) At half past nine we have a group .arriving (arrive) from Leonidas Tours.
(c) At a quarter to ten. I'm meeting. (meet) Robert Blye, of Servex Hotel Equipment.
(d) From .... till .... the Lea Social Club ..... (hold) its Annual General Meeting.
(e) At .... I ...... (make) a speech for the Head Porter's long-service award.
(f) From .... till .... we have delegates .... (check in) for the Insurance Conference.
(g) Then at .... we ...... the opening of the Insurance Conference.
(h) And from .... till .... we have the Rio Disco Party in the basement.

11 Cover up the sentences you completed. Use the diary entries to talk about the Assistant Manager's day to your partner.

Follow-up

12 Work with a partner.

Student A
Take the part of the tourists, holidaymakers and businessmen you heard in Exercise 7. (You can use your own words, or any words you can remember from the

5

exercise.) Tell the clerk in the Information Bureau your needs so that he can recommend a suitable hotel for you.

Student B
Take the part of the clerk in the Information Bureau. Listen to the people who come to you. Recommend a suitable hotel. (You can use the hotels advertised in Exercise 6, or talk about other hotels if you like.) Say why you think the hotel is suitable.

13 Work with a partner.

Student A
You are the Assistant Manager. Write your 'diary' for the day — the events, meetings and arrivals that are due to take place in the hotel. Then telephone the Reception Clerk and tell him what he needs to know.

Student B
You are the Reception Clerk. You want to know what it happening in the hotel to-day. You are discussing the timetable with the Assistant Manager. Make a note of the information the Assistant Manager gives you. Ask questions as necessary.

14 Work with a partner. Student A reads the information below. Student B reads the information on page 182.

Student A
You are secretary to the Hotel Manager. You are telling him about the events that are due to take place, listed below. For example, you might say:

We have a group of a hundred Japanese tourists *arriving* at nine thirty.
A salesman from the telephone company *is coming* to demonstrate new switchboard equipment at ten thirty.

9.30.   100 Japanese tourists   arrive
10.30. Salesman from telephone company (to demonstrate new switch board equipment)
12.15. Assistant Manager leaves by train for National Hotel Conference.
14.00. Minister of Education from San Bernardo arrives
15.45. Interviews for new Reception Clerk

Unfortunately, the Manager has also made arrangements that he has not told you about. Discuss the timetable for the day, and help in deciding what to do.

Language reference

Types of hotel: resort hotel; commercial hotel; congress hotel; motel; airport hotel; guest house; country house hotel; luxury hotel; inn; one-star hotel; two-star hotel; etc.

Expressions of location: situated in; near the sea; in a town centre; in pleasant scenery; in a quiet place; (two) minutes from; located in; close to; centrally located; attractively set (beside); with views of; surrounded by; in the heart of; overlooking; midway between; famous for.

Other characteristics: built specially to provide a certain kind of service; provides facilities for ...; provides accommodation for ...; offers ....

Expressing times on the clock

Written forms: 01.00; 11.30; 14.45; 19.30; 21.15; etc. May also be written as: 1.00 am; 11.30 am; 2.45 pm; 7.30 pm; 9.15 pm, etc.

Spoken forms: The above forms would probably be said as *one o'clock (in the morning)*, *eleven thirty (in the morning)*, *two forty-five (in the afternoon)*, *seven thirty (in the evening)*, *nine fifteen (at night)*. But *am* and *pm* can be used in speech also — one *am*, two forty-five *pm*, etc. It is also possible to use the forms *half-past eleven* (for 11.30, etc.), *a quarter to three* (for 14.45, etc.), *a quarter past nine* (for 21.15, etc.).

Note: In America, forms like *a quarter of two* can be heard (for 01.45) or *a quarter after two* (for 02.15).

Talking about arrangements for the day

For arranged events, the present continuous is common:

A salesman *is giving* a demonstration at eleven thirty.

But in a hotel, *have* would often be used, like this:

We have a wedding party this afternoon.

We have a large group *arriving* this afternoon.

Making a decision

Simple future: *We'll put* them in a different room, etc.

Use of *have to*: *We'll have to* put them in a different room, etc.

Miscellaneous vocabulary

accommodation	facility	relax
adequate	furnishings	resort
celebration	guest house	scale
clarify	informal	scenery
coach	inn	service
commercial	international	situated

7

conference	luxury	spacious
congress	moderate	standard
due to	motel	wealthy
entertainment	motorist	wedding
exhibition	recreation	

UNIT 2

Hotel staff

To start you off

1 Hotels can be organized in different ways, and the names of jobs and departments vary from hotel to hotel. But there are certain departments that you will find in most hotels. Match the places on the left with the words on the right.

(a) where guests make reservations, check in
and check out
(b) where guests eat
(c) where guests drink alcoholic or soft drinks
(d) where food is cooked
(e) where bills are added up and money
matters dealt with
(f) the department that makes sure the hotel
and the rooms are clean, and that
everything in the rooms is in order

    (i) Housekeeping
   (ii) Kitchen
  (iii) Restaurant
  (iv) Front Office or Reception
   (v) Bar
  (vi) Cashier's office

2 Check if you know words for the following jobs. Often there is more than one word that can be used.

(a) The person responsible for the cooking in the kitchens.
(b) The person who looks after guests' reservations.
(c) The person in charge of service to guests in the restaurant.
(d) The person responsible for keeping the hotel clean and supplying linen.
(e) The person who looks after all money paid to or by the hotel.
(f) The person responsible for greeting guests, helping them with their luggage,
organizing their transport, and dealing with their mail.

3 Complete these sentences, spoken by a hotel manager. You will hear them in the Listening exercise. Use these words:

    responsible under (× 3) charge after includes to supervises

(a) The Assistant Manager is _____ for the day-to-day running of the hotel.

(b) We have three receptionists who work _____ the Head Receptionist.
(c) In this hotel, the Head Porter reports _____ the Head Receptionist.
(d) The Head Housekeeper is in _____ of the chambermaids and cleaners.
(e) We have four bar operatives, looking _____ the bars in the hotel.
(f) The bars and the restaurants all come _____ the responsibility of the Restaurant Manager. The Restaurant Section _____ both restaurant and bar service.
(g) The Head Waiter _____ three Station Waiters, and two part-time waiters.
(h) _____ the Head Chef we have the Second Chef, and two trainee chefs.

Developing the topic

4 A student from a Hotel College is interviewing a Hotel Manager for a project she is doing. Check your answers to Exercise 3. Then listen again and label the diagram below where you see the letters (a)–(h).

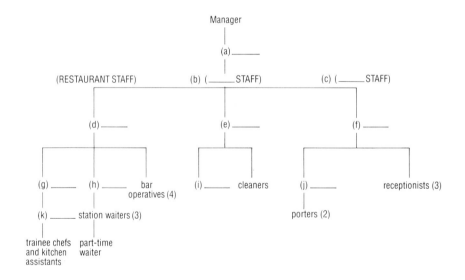

5 Ask and answer questions about the staff in the diagram you labelled:

What	does	the Manager	do?
Who	do	Assistant Manager	look after?
		Head Chef	supervise?
		Head Housekeeper	work under?

What		the Head Receptionist	
Who		Head Chef	
	is	Head Porter	in charge of?
	are	Head Waiter	responsible for?
		Bar Operatives	
		Chambermaids	

He	look(s) after ...	
She	supervise(s) ...	
They	work(s) under ...	
	is	in charge of ...
	are	responsible for ...

6 Look at the pictures below. They show some hotel workers. What jobs do they do? Write the name of the job below each picture.

Make sentences about the pictures, giving reasons for your answers. This table will help you:

I	know	he	is a _____	because	he	is talking to . . .
	think	she			she	wearing . . .
						helping . . .
						using . . .
						etc.

7 Find out what the following people do. Then write sentences using *look after, supervise, in charge of, responsible for, work under,* or any suitable verb.

Key Clerk   Chambermaid   Night Clerk   Hall Porter   Head Porter
Switchboard Operator   Floor Attendant   Storekeeper   Maintenance Engineer
Waiter's Assistant   Sous Chef   Valet   Concierge

(a) ....

(b) ....

(c) ....

(d) ....

(e) ....

(f) ....

(g) ....

(h) ....

(i) ....

(j) ....

(k) ....

(l) ....

(m) ....

8 Listen to the hotel guests talking to the receptionist on duty about various needs they have. Which member of the hotel staff could help them? Stop the tape when instructed, and write in the names of hotel staff below.

Guest 1: _____   Guest 5: _____
Guest 2: _____   Guest 6: _____
Guest 3: _____   Guest 7: _____
Guest 4: _____   Guest 8: _____

9 Listen to the complete conversations between the guests and the Receptionist on duty. Check your answers to Exercise 8. Then complete the sentences used by the Receptionist, below:

1. If you talk to the _____ he'll ....
2. No problem, sir. The _____ will ....
3. Certainly sir. I'll talk to the _____ and she'll ....
4. I'm sorry about that, sir. I'll contact the _____ at once and find out
    ....
5. We'll soon arrange that for you madam. The _____ will ....
    ....
6. I'm terribly sorry, madam. I'll call the _____ at once. He'll ....
    ....
7. Yes sir. The _____ over there ....
8. If you'd like to sit down a moment, I'll tell the _____. He'll ......
    ....

10 Look at the organization chart below. Make sentences about hotel staff — the people or departments they *look after, supervise, work under*, etc.

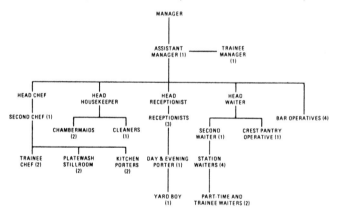

Follow-up

11 Work with a partner. Act out any of the conversations you can remember from Exercise 9 (listening). If you wish, you can add additional needs which the Receptionist giving advice must reply to.

12 Work with a partner.

Student A
You have spoken to the Receptionist. Now talk to the member of the hotel staff who is available to help you. Explain your needs to him/her.

Student B
You are the member of the hotel staff who can help the guest. Listen to his/her

needs. Either (a) offer to help, or (b) explain why you are unable to help at the moment.

13 Work with a partner

YOU draw a diagram to show the organization of any hotel you know or can imagine. Do not show the diagram to anyone else.

YOU describe the organization in the diagram to your partner, or to other students in your class.

YOUR PARTNER or OTHER STUDENTS try to draw and label a diagram of the organization you have described, from your description.

When you have finished, compare the diagrams the other students have drawn with your original diagram.

14 Play a game, like this:

YOU think of any job that is done in a hotel. Pretend you do the job. Ask other students 'What's my job?'.

OTHER STUDENTS ask yes/no questions about the job. You can only answer 'yes' or 'no'. They must try to guess the job you do in ten questions or less.

Language reference

Hotel staff

Some managerial positions
General Manager
Assistant General Manager
Duty Manager (= the person acting as manager at a particular time)
Personnel Manager, House Manager, Catering Manager, Banqueting Manager, etc.

Reception/Front Office
Front Office Manager/Reception Manager
Receptionist/Reception Clerk
Reservations Clerk
Room Clerk/Key Clerk
Telephonist/Switchboard Operator
Night Clerk

Housekeeping
Housekeeper

Floor Maid/Floor Attendant
Room Maid/Chambermaid
Cleaner
Laundry Maid
Concierge

Hall Porter's Department
(Head) Hall Porter (= Bell Captain, Am.E.)
Porter (= Bellboy/Bellhop, Am.E.)
Doorman
Pageboy
Lift Attendant/Lift Boy (= Elevator Operator, Am.E.)
Valet
Cloakroom Attendant
Enquiries Clerk
Night Porter

Cashier's department
Hotel Controller
Accountant
Cashier

Food and Beverage Department
Maître d'hotel
Waiter (Head Waiter, Station Waiter, Wine Waiter, Lounge Waiter)
Waiter's assistant (= Busboy/busser, Am.E.)
Chef (Head Chef, Chef de cuisine, Commis Chef, etc.)
Bar Operative/Barman (= Bartender, Am.E.)

Miscellaneous
Maintenance Engineer
Storekeeper/Storeman

Terms to indicate rank
head (as in head waiter)
second, etc. (as in second chef)
manager (as in reception manager)
supervisor (as in breakfast supervisor)
assistant (as in assistant housekeeper)
senior (as in senior telephonist)
junior (as in junior receptionist)

French terms used to describe kitchen and restaurant staff
chef de cuisine (= 'head of the kitchen')
sous chef (= 'under chef'; deputy to the chef de cuisine)

chef de parties (responsible for a kitchen department, e.g. vegetable preparation)
commis chef (= junior cook)
maître d'hôtel (= head waiter)
chef de rangs (= skilled station waiter)
commis de rangs (= assistant waiter)

Structures and expressions used in describing departments and duties
X is responsible for Y
X is in charge of Y
X looks after Y
X comes under Y
X works under Y
X reports to Y
X supervises Y
X includes Y

Simple present to describe job activities
The chambermaids work under the direction of the housekeeper, etc.

Simple future to promise help from a particular member of staff
The porter will take your luggage ..., etc.

Miscellaneous vocabulary

convention	part-time
deal with	responsibility
greet	trainee
linen	various
organize	vary

Room types

To start you off

1 Without looking at the rest of the page, how many types of hotel room can you think of?

2 Do you know words for the following types of room? Match these definitions with the words underneath.

(a) A room occupied by one person.
(b) A room with one large bed for two people.
(c) A room with two single beds for two people.
(d) A room with three single beds, or a double bed and a single bed, suitable for occupation by three people.
(e) A set of two or more rooms including a bedroom and a sitting room.
(f) A large room with a partition to separate the bedroom area from the sitting room area.
(g) A well-furnished and luxurious suite at the top of the building.
(h) A room with four or more beds, particularly suitable for a family with children.
(i) A room not used as a bedroom, where guests may read, watch television, etc.
(j) Two or more rooms with a door to allow access from one room to another.

1. SUITE
2. FAMILY ROOM
3. TWIN ROOM
4. SINGLE ROOM
5. PENTHOUSE
6. CONNECTING or ADJOINING ROOMS
7. DOUBLE ROOM
8. TRIPLE ROOM
9. JUNIOR SUITE
10. LOUNGE or SITTING ROOM
(or PARLOR, = Am.E.)

3 Complete these sentences spoken by a hotel manager answering enquiries about rooms. You will hear them in Exercise 5.

(a) All our rooms have c__ __ tr __l h__ __t__ng.
(b) They all have a w__sh b__ __in and a t__ __l__t.

(c) Our single rooms are very c__mf__rt__b__ __ and the rates are very r__ason__b__ __.

(d) Or for real ec__n__my, let's suppose you have a sales conference. You could d__ __ble up your sales staff and put them into t__ __n rooms.

(e) For something more l__x__r__ous, we can offer our Delphos Suite.

(f) It has its own private t__rr__ __e, where guests can sit outside and enjoy the view over the lake.

(g) I can recommend our Bella Vista Penthouse. From the b__lc__ __y there's a magnificent view over the whole countryside.

4 What kinds of room do these pictures show?

1

2

3

4

Developing the topic

🔊

5 A secretary from Speed Sportswear is talking to the Manager of the Park Hotel, to arrange accommodation for visiting staff. Accommodation will be needed for all grades, from sales staff to Managing Directors.

Listen to the conversation and check your answers to Exercise 3. Then listen again and answer these questions:

(a) Will Speed Sportswear have to pay normal room rates? How do you know?
(b) In the opinion of the Hotel Manager, what kind of staff would the following room types be suitable for, and why?
    — the single rooms
    — the twin rooms
    — the Delphos Suite
    — the Bella Vista Penthouse

🔊

6 Listen again. Fill in the normal 'rack' rates for the room types mentioned in the conversation.

```
PARK HOTEL — DAILY ROOM RATES

Single room        _____
Double room        _____
Twin room          _____
Triple room      £70.00
Family room      £85.00
Junior suite     £105.00
'Delphos' ground floor suite      _____
'Bella Vista' penthouse suite     _____
```

7 In pairs practise asking and answering questions about room types, using the following:

Can you provide suitable accommodation for	company directors? managers? staff with their families? salespeople? trainees? married couples? etc.

Certainly, you'll find our	single rooms twin rooms double rooms family rooms ground floor suite penthouse suite etc.	suitable.	They have ... It has ... etc. *(say why the room type is suitable)*

8 Most hotels contain rooms which are used for purposes other than accommodation. Match the rooms on the left with the purposes on the right.

(a) Banquet Room   (i) for showing goods and products
(b) Ballroom   (ii) for holding large-scale meetings
(c) Reception Room   (iii) for dancing
(d) Conference Room   (iv) for cocktail parties and social events
(e) Exhibition Room   (v) for a large group eating a special meal

9 Listen to enquiries from five people who need rooms in a hotel. Stop the tape when instructed. What kind of room (or rooms) would you offer them?

Enquiry 1 ....   Enquiry 4 ....
Enquiry 2 ....   Enquiry 5 ....
Enquiry 3 ....

10 Listen to the next part of the tape. You can hear the suggestions the Receptionist makes, but they are not in the same order as the enquiries above. Match suggestions and enquiries.

Suggestion (1) goes with Enquiry __
Suggestion (2) goes with Enquiry __
Suggestion (3) goes with Enquiry __
Suggestion (4) goes with Enquiry __
Suggestion (5) goes with Enquiry __

Now work with a partner and try to act out the conversations between the people making enquiries and the receptionist.

Follow-up

11 Read the following sentences to your partner (whose book should be closed).

You can read the sentences in any order. Your partner should say as quickly as possible what the sentence refers to. Add more sentences of your own.

(a) It's a room with one large bed for two people.
(b) It's a room where you can show goods and products to people who are interested in them.
(c) It's a room where you can have a meeting for a large number of people.
(d) It's a place where you can stand or sit, built out from the window of an upstairs room.
(e) It's a large vertical section of wood or plastic that divides two parts of a room.
(f) It's a room with a door which leads through to another room.
(g) It's an area outside a room, in the open air, where guests can sit and have a drink or a meal.
(h) It's a room where a lot of people can dance.
(i) It's a system that takes heat from one place and supplies it to all the rooms in the hotel.
(j) It's an item of soft furniture that people sit on or sometimes sleep on.

12 Work with a group of students. You are in a partnership which has just bought a large hotel. You are reorganizing the rooms in the hotel, and adding many new features. Draw up a list of 'special' rooms in you hotel (not just ordinary bedrooms). Decide on their names, their special features, and the rate for occupying them.

13 Work with a student from *another* group.

Student A
You are a manager in the hotel you reorganized in the previous exercise. Be ready to answer enquiries about the hotel from people with special needs.

Student B
Take the part of three or four people with special needs who require rooms. Explain your needs to the manager, and find out what he/she can offer.

14 For Student A's part, see below. For Student B's part see page 182.

Student A
You own a hotel. You want to improve the hotel by adding:
— four double/twin rooms
— a ground floor suite, with terrace
— a conference room
— an exhibition room

You can afford to pay £360,000 at most. You are discussing your plans with a building (Student B), who is giving his estimate for how much your plans would cost.

Note down the builder's estimates. Calculate the total cost and make a final decision about the extra rooms you want. Tell the builder what you want him to do.

Language reference

Names of rooms

single	sitting room/parlor (Am. E.)/lounge
double	connecting/adjoining rooms
twin	banquet room
triple	ballroom
family	reception room
suite	conference room
junior suite	exhibition/display room
penthouse	

Miscellaneous vocabulary

access	partition
accommodation	reasonable
balcony	sofa
central heating	staff
connected	storey
convertible	terrace
economy	toilet
grade	trainee
luxurious	view
magnificent	well-furnished

UNIT 4

Room furnishings and equipment

To start you off

1 Look at the pictures below of a bedroom and a bathroom. Can you say what the items in the pictures are?

2 Find jobs that a chambermaid does. Match words in the columns below. Usually, more than one verb is possible.

replace, wipe, vacuum, make, change, water empty, clean, polish, dust	the plants, the bed, the mirror the floor, the towels, the toilet, desk tops and table top, the bath the carpets, the sheets, the ashtray

3 Look at the pictures below. What is the chambermaid doing in each picture?

Developing the topic

4 Listen to the guests who are mentioning problems with their rooms. Stop the tape when instructed. Complete what the guests say, below.

Guest (1). The _____ in my _____ _____ is _____.
Guest (2). There's no _____ _____ in this _____.
Guest (3). The _____ haven't been _____.
Guest (4). The _____ in my room is _____ _____.

Guest (5). The _____ is very _____.
Guest (6). The _____ needs _____.
Guest (7). There are _____ _____ in the _____.
Guest (8). The _____ hasn't been _____.

How would *you* reply to Guests 1–8 above?

[QO]

5 Listen to the replies to the guests in the previous exercise. They are not in the same order. Match the replies with the number of each guest.

Reply A goes with Guest __.	Reply E goes with Guest __.
Reply B goes with Guest __.	Reply F goes with Guest __.
Reply C goes with Guest __.	Reply G goes with Guest __.
Reply D goes with Guest __.	Reply H goes with Guest __.

6 Practise with a partner using sentences like those in the tables below.

Student 1	There's There are	no toilet paper no soap no towels no sheets telephone directory room service menu television coathangers etc.	in on	the	room. washbasin. bed. desk. bathroom. bedroom. wardrobe. etc.
Student 2	Sorry sir/madam, I'll		bring	one some	up for you.

Student 1	The bed sheets bath wastepaper basket etc.		hasn't been haven't been	made. changed. cleaned. emptied. etc.
Student 2	I'm sorry about that, I'll send someone up to	make change clean empty etc.	it them	right away.

Student 1	The	bath	needs	cleaning.			
		sheets	need	changing.			
		etc.		etc.			

Student 2	I'm terribly sorry, sir/madam.	I'll ask the Chambermaid to come up and	clean change etc.	it them	at once.

7 In every room, the Housekeeper or Chambermaid has to check for items that may be damaged, missing, etc. Which items do you think may be:

(a) broken?   (d) marked, or stained?
(b) missing?   (e) out of order?
(c) torn?

8 Listen to a trainee chambermaid discussing with the floor maid items which are damaged, missing, etc. Write notes in the table below.

ROOM	NATURE OF DAMAGE, etc.	ACTION ALREADY TAKEN	ACTION TO BE TAKEN NOW
101			
201			
301			
401			

9 With a partner, ask and answer questions from the tables below:

Student 1

Have you	replaced reported cleaned etc.	the broken light bulb/window/mirror, etc.? the missing towel/ashtray, etc.? the torn sheet/telephone directory, etc.? the cigarette burn on the bedspread/carpet, etc.? the stained desk top/bath, etc.? the faulty TV set/radio, etc.? the dirty lampshade/curtain, etc.?

Student 2

Yes, I've already	replaced etc.	it.
Not yet, but I'm going to	replace etc.	it now.

Follow-up

10 Point to items in the pictures on page 23. Ask your partner 'What's this?'. Your partner must answer as quickly as possible.

OR

Say the names of items in the pictures, in mixed order. Your partner must point to the items in the pictures, as quickly as possible.

11 Play a guessing game, like this:

YOU think of any item in the pictures on page 23.
OTHER STUDENTS ask 'yes/no' questions. For example:
  Does it need replacing very often?
  Is it something you clean every day?
  Does it get torn?, etc.
YOU answer 'Yes' or 'No' to each question.
OTHER STUDENTS try to guess the item in no more than seven questions.

12 Work with a partner.

Student 1
You are a Housekeeper reporting to a Hotel Manager on the state of a room after a guest has left it. A lot of things have been damaged and a lot of things are missing.

Student 2
You are the Hotel Manager. Ask the Housekeeper questions, to find out exactly how much is damaged or missing. Take a note of the information the Housekeeper gives. Decide what you are going to do about it.

13 For Student A's part, see below. For Student B's part see page 182.

Student A
You are a trainee housekeeper. You are contacting the hotel Maintenance Engineer (Student B) to tell him about:

— a TV set that is out of order in room 302
— a telephone that is out of order in room 221
— a water pipe that is leaking in room 119
— a window that cannot be shut in room 120
— two bulbs that need replacing in the second floor corridor

Find out:
(a) if the Maintenance Engineer will attend to the jobs
(b) when the jobs will be done
(c) what he wants you to do yourself

Imagine that your teacher is the Chief Housekeeper. Report to your teacher what the Maintenance Engineer has told you.

Language reference

Items of furniture and equipment in bedroom and bathroom

ashtray	plug	toilet
bedside table	radiator	toilet flush
blanket	reading lamp	toilet paper
bulb	set	towel
chair	sheet	TV
coat hanger	shower	venetian blind
curtains	shower curtain	wall cabinet
desk	tap (= faucet, Am. E.)	wardrobe
desk top	telephone	wastepaper basket
hotel stationery	telephone directory	

Verbs of cleaning and housekeeping

clean	replace
wipe	vacuum
brush	wipe
dust	water (a plant)
empty	

Present perfect to check on jobs done
Have you replaced the missing bulb?, etc.

Going to for intended actions
I'm going to report it now, etc.

***Will* for promises**
I'll send someone up immediately, etc.

***Need* + ... *ing* to describe requirements**
The plant needs watering every two days, etc.

Talking about missing items
There's no ..... ; There are no .....

Pronouns *one* and *some*
I'll bring one/some right away.

'Damage' adjectives
broken; damaged; faulty; marked; missing; out of order; stained; torn

Miscellaneous vocabulary

cigarette burn	right away
corridor	rust
immediately	satisfied
leak	thorough
maintenance	unpack
report	

UNIT 5

Room rates

To start you off

1 Look at the brochure below. Answer these questions as quickly as possible.

(a) Which hotel is the cheapest? Which is the most expensive?
(b) In which hotels do all the rooms have a bathroom?
(c) In which months do the rates below apply?
(d) In which hotel can children stay free in the same room as their parents?
(e) Which hotels include breakfast in the room rate?
(f) Which hotel quotes an inclusive rate for dinner, bed and breakfast?
(g) Which hotel quotes only rates per person?
(h) In which hotel is there the smallest difference between the price of a single room and the price of a double room?
(i) Find a word meaning 'room rates'.

HOTELS IN MIDFORD

(June-September; tariffs include service and VAT)

THE PHOENIX HOTEL
Single room £16, with bath £20. Double room £28, with bath £35; Breakfast £5 per person; children under 12, 50% reduction.

THE PARK HOTEL
Bed and breakfast per person £16; Double room with bath £25; Dinner bed and breakfast £29 full board.

THE DALTON HOTEL
Single room with bath £30, Double room with bath £60: children under 12 in same room as parents free: breakfast £6 per person.

THE CASTLE INN
Single room £12, Double Room £15. Includes continental breakfast (English breakfast £3 extra).

2 Complete these sentences. You will hear them spoken to a foreign tourist in Exercise 3.

(a) (The Castle Inn) The price includes continental breakfast. If you want a full _____ breakfast you'll have to pay extra.
(b) (The Dalton Hotel) There is no _____ for children under 12 who _____ in the same room as their parents.

(c) (The Park Hotel) There's a rate of £25 which _____ dinner, bed and breakfast.

(d) (The Park Hotel) The rates quoted for this hotel are per person, not _____
_____.

(e) (The Phoenix Hotel) It will _____ you £20 for a _____ room with
_____.

(f) These are the rates for June _____ September. You would pay _____
at other times of the year.

Developing the topic

3 Listen to the conversation between a clerk in a Hotel Reservations Bureau and a tourist. Check your answers to Exercise 2. Then listen again and answer these questions:

(a) What is full board?
(b) What is half board?
(c) What is a continental breakfast?
(d) What is an English breakfast?
(e) How much service charge is included in these prices?
(f) What do the letters VAT stand for?

4 Complete the dialogues below about the hotels on page 30.

1.
A: How much does a single room in the Castle Inn cost?
B: ....
A: ....?
B: Yes, it includes continental breakfast.
A: ....?
B: You'll have to pay £3 extra.

2.
A: How much is a room at the Dalton Hotel?
B: ....?
A: Double.
B: ....
A: ....?
B: Children stay free if they are in the same room as their parents.

3.
A: ....?
B: £16 per person.

31

A: ....?
B: Yes, there's a bath in every room.
A: ....
B: Yes, you can get half board for £25, and full board for £29.

4.
A: ....?
B: £35.
A: ....?
B: Yes. For a double room alone you'd pay £28.
A: ....?
B: No. Breakfast is £5 extra.
A: ....?
B: Yes. There's a reduction of 50% for children under 12.

5 With a partner, ask and answer questions about the hotels on page 30, or any other hotels you or your partner know about. For example:

How much is a (single/double) room in ...... (*name of a hotel*)?
Is that with bath?
Does that include breakfast?
Is there a rate for half board/full board?
Is there a reduction for children?

6 A secretary in a company is talking to the Manager of the Valley Hotel to find out the weekly rates. Listen, and fill in the table below.

```
VALLEY HOTEL — WEEKLY RATES
(ACCOMMODATION IN SINGLE ROOM WITH BATH)
.............. Plan:    £150
.............. Plan:    £165
.............. Plan:    £195
.............. Plan:    £220
```

7 There are several names for the 'plans' you have heard about in this unit. Match the words and definitions in the columns below. You can check your answers in the Language Reference section.

1. Half board   A. En pension
2. Full board   B. Demi-pension
3. Bed and breakfast
4. Room only

(a)	Continental plan	(i)	room with no meals included
(b)	Modified American plan	(ii)	room + breakfast + one other meal
(c)	European plan	(iii)	room + all meals
(d)	American plan	(iv)	room + breakfast

Follow-up

8 Draw up a list of rates for rooms and food plans for a hotel (it could be a hotel you know, or an imaginary hotel).

Student A
Act the part of a reception clerk, giving information when asked.

Student B
Act the part of a tourist who is planning a holiday and who wants to find out about rooms and rates in Student A's hotel.

9 Look at these advertisements for accommodation in south-west England.

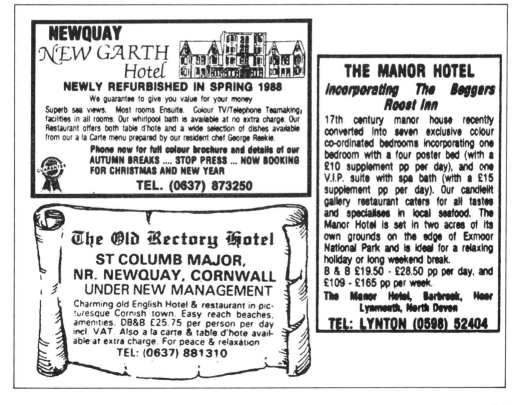

Student A

You are a tourist who is enquiring about hotels in a Hotel Reservations Bureau. Do not look at the advertisements above. Obtain information about the hotels from Student B. Tell B to make a booking for you in one of the hotels.

Student B

You work in a Hotel Reservations Bureau. Answer A's questions. Use information from the advertisements above if possible. Take instructions from A about the hotel and the type of room he/she wants you to book.

10   Work with a partner. For Student A's part see below. For Student B's part see page 183.

Student A

You are a retired shopkeeper. Your hobbies are going for long walks and bird-watching. You haven't got a great amount of money to spend on your holiday, but you are not interested in luxurious living in any case, and you like to have peace and quiet.

You would like to stay for a few days in a pleasant seaside town where you could easily walk along the coast — but you haven't made up your mind how long you will stay. You are finding out from the Reservations Clerk at the Cliff Hotel whether the rates and the style of accommodation there will suit you. Ask questions as necessary, and decide whether you want to stay at the hotel, and for how long.

Language reference

Expressions used in quoting rates: for a single/double room;   per person/room; the price includes . . . .

Nouns of cost: the room rate(s);   the tariff(s);   a supplement;   service charge; VAT;   a reduction (of 50% etc);   a discount.

Verbs of cost: the room costs £x;   the hotel charges £x for a room;   it will cost you £x for a room.

Meals

English breakfast: a breakfast including cooked food, offering for example porridge, fried bacon, fried egg, sausages, etc.

Continental breakfast: a breakfast consisting of tea or coffee and baked produce (bread, buns, rolls, croissants, toast) with butter and jam, honey or marmalade.

Lunch.

Dinner.

Food plans

European plan: the rate for a room alone, with no meals included at all.

Bed and breakfast/continental plan: the rate includes the room and breakfast. (The breakfast itself may be 'English' or 'continental'.)

Half board/demi-pension/modified American plan: this includes the room, plus breakfast and one other meal (lunch or dinner).

Full board/en pension/American plan: room and all meals included.

Hotel reservations (1) By telephone and face to face

To start you off

1 Bill Jackson is telephoning the Palace Hotel to make a reservation.

What might he say? What might the Reception Clerk say? Give examples.

2 When reserving a room, most customers are not as efficient and concise as this:

'I'd like to reserve a single room with bathroom en suite for tomorrow night, staying for three nights, at £25 a night. My name is Bill Jackson and I'll be arriving around nine o'clock.'

However, the conversation between the customer and the Reception Clerk will probably deal with the same points.

Work with another student. How could you make Bill Jackson's reservation more realistic? What information would Bill Jackson give himself? What information would the clerk ask for? Deal with these points:

(a) wish to make a reservation
(b) type of room
(c) length of stay
(d) room rate
(e) name of guest
(f) time of arrival

3 Complete the following sentences, spoken by the Reception Clerk to another customer. You will hear them in Exercise 4.

(a) Yes madam. Single, double or _____?
(b) And how many _____ are you planning to stay, madam?
(c) We can give you a twin room with _____ en suite for £40 a _____, _____ breakfast. Would that be _____?
(d) And the _____, please?
(e) And do you know what _____ you'll be arriving, madam?

Developing the topic

4 Listen to the dialogue again. Check your answers to Exercise 3. Then fill in the table below.

RESERVATION FORM

Name of customer: _____   Room type: _____

Date of arrival: _____   Room rate: _____

Length of stay: _____   Time of arrival: _____

---

5 Practise with a partner using ideas from this table. Change details of the room type, length of stay, etc. according to your own ideas. You can join several ideas together if you wish.

THE CUSTOMER MIGHT ...	THE RESERVATIONS CLERK MIGHT ...
wish to reserve a room: I'd like to reserve a room for 21st January, etc.	*ask about the type of room needed:* Yes sir. For how many? Single, double or twin? Would you like a room with bathroom en suite? etc.
say the type of room: ... a single room, please ... a twin room with bathroom, etc.	
say the length of stay: ... for three nights, etc.	*ask about length of stay:* How many nights?
	offer a room: We can give you a twin room with bathroom en suite ... etc.
ask about the room rate: Can you tell me how much it would be?	*... at a certain rate:* (for) £30 a night including breakfast, etc.
say the rate or type is suitable: That would be fine.	*... and ask if that will be suitable* Would that be suitable?
say name: George Sanderson	*ask the guest's name:* And the name please?
say time of arrival: Probably around 9 o'clock.	*ask time of arrival:* Do you know what time you'll be arriving, sir?
	confirm reservation, welcome, etc.: Thank you sir. I've reserved the room for you. We look forward to seeing you.

6 When asking questions, it is sometimes more polite to include an indirect form (see Language Reference section). Change the following questions to include an indirect form. Begin with the words in brackets.

(a) What kind of room would your director prefer? (Can you tell me ...?)
(b) How many nights will you be staying? (Do you know ...?)
(c) Would a twin room with bathroom at £35 be suitable? (Do you think ...?)

(d) What time will you be arriving? (Have you any idea . . .?)
(e) When will you be checking out? (Do you know . . .?)
(f) What kind of transport will Mr Jones require? (Do you know . . .?)
(g) How many would there be in your group? (Can you tell me . . .?)

7 It is sometimes more polite to use continuous forms of the verb when asking questions, rather than simple forms (see Language Reference section). What questions can you ask in the following situations:

(a) Before you accept the reservation, you want to know how long the guest would stay. (How long . . .?)
(b) When the guest is in the hotel, you want to know if he will leave tomorrow as planned. (Will . . ., sir?)
(c) After you have accepted the reservation, you want to know what time the guest will arrive. (What time . . ., madam?)
(d) Before you accept a reservation for a group, you want to know how many would arrive on Thursday night. (How many . . .?)
(e) When a guest arrives for one night, you want to know if she will require transport to the airport tomorrow. (Will . . ., madam?)
(f) Before you accept a reservation, you want to know if the person would have all his meals in the hotel. (Would . . ., sir?)

8 Look at the notes on dates in the Language Reference section. How would you say these dates?

21/1/91	May 19 1995	3rd May 1996
4 Sept 89	1.12.99 (British usage)	12 Nov 97
6/2/91 (British usage)	1.12.99 (American usage)	October 2nd 1998
6/2/91 (American usage)	23 Feb 93	4-3-2001 (American usage)

9 Listen to the three dialogues on the tape. Answer these questions:

(a) In which dialogue does a person want a single room? a double room? a twin room?
(b) In which dialogue is a person staying one night? two nights? four nights?
(c) In which dialogue does a person want to say in the hotel from tonight? the day after tomorrow? 4th September?
(d) In which dialogues do the customers ask about the room rate?
(e) In which dialogues does the clerk check on suitability?

10 Listen again. Match the expressions you hear in the dialogues with the ideas below. Write down the expressions you hear.

The customer wishes to reserve a room.

Dialogue 1 ....
Dialogue 2 ....
Dialogue 3 ....

The clerk asks about the type of room needed.

Dialogue 1 ....
Dialogue 2 ....
Dialogue 3 ....

The clerk asks about length of stay.

Dialogue 1 ....
Dialogue 2 ....
Dialogue 3 ....

The clerk offers a particular type of room.

Dialogue 1 ....
Dialogue 2 ....
Dialogue 3 ....

The clerk asks about suitability.

Dialogue 1 ....
Dialogue 3 ....

The clerk talks about the room rate.

Dialogue 1 ....
Dialogue 2 ....
Dialogue 3 ....

The clerk asks the customer's name.

Dialogue 1 ....
Dialogue 2 ....
Dialogue 3 ....

The clerk repeats the reservation details, welcomes the customer, etc.

Dialogue 1 ....
Dialogue 2 ....
Dialogue 3 ....

Follow-up

11 **Student A** 'Telephone' Student B to make a reservation. Be ready to give details of the dates and the type of room you need. Find out what Student B can offer you. Decide whether to make a firm reservation or not.

Student B You are a Reservations Clerk. You are unable to give Student A *exactly* what he/she wants, but you can offer an alternative. For example, you can offer:

(a) the dates he/she wants, but with a different type of room, or
(b) the room type he/she wants, but for different dates

Thus, you might say:
'I'm sorry. We don't have a double room from the first to the fifth of June, but we do have a twin room at £50 a night.'
'I'm sorry. We don't have a double room from the first to the fifth of June, but we do have one available from the second to the fifth of June, and we can offer you a twin room for the first night' (offer different possibilities according to your own ideas).

Take A's reservation if he/she decides to make a firm reservation.

12 With a partner, try to act out any dialogue from the previous section.

13 With a partner, practise making and responding to these requests:

(a) Do you have a double room for tomorrow night, please?
(b) What's the difference in price between a twin room and a double room?
(c) I don't sleep very well, so I'd like a quiet room, please.
(d) Can you give me a room with a view of the lake?
(e) What's your cheapest room, please?
(f) Can you put in an extra bed in the room for a child of eight?
(g) Is it the same price for a twin room and a double room?

14 Work with a partner. For Student A's part, see below. For Student B's part see page 183.

Student A
You want to book a room for yourself, your wife and your son, aged eight. You would like a room with bathroom, but you would not like to pay more than £45 per night. You would like to stay for four nights.

Language reference

The customer says:

Requesting a reservation
Have you got a room ...?;   I'd like to reserve/book a room ...;   Can I reserve
a room ...?

The Reception Clerk says:

Asking about room type
For how many?;   Is that a single room, sir?;   Single, double or twin room?
  Would you like a room with bathroom en suite?;   With bathroom (or without)?,
  etc.

Asking about length of stay
(For) how many nights?;   How many nights are you planning to stay?;   How many
  nights will you be staying?

Offering a room
We can give you a (single room) at (£50 a night)

Asking about suitability
Would that be suitable?;   Would that suit you?

Asking about the name
(And) the name, please?;   And your name is ...?;   What was the name, please?;
  And could I have your name, please?

Asking about time of arrival
What time will/would you be arriving?;   Do you know what time you'll be arriving?

Expressing agreement, willingness or understanding
(rather formal) Very good sir;   (less formal) That's fine, sir

Confirming reservation
Thank you sir/madam. I've reserved Room 123 for you;   The room number is
  456;   That's a (single room) at (£50 a night)

Welcoming to the hotel
We look forward to seeing you;   We look forward to having you with us

Apologizing and offering an alternative
I'm sorry. We don't have a (single room with bathroom) from the (third to the
  fourth of May), but we do have a (single room with shower) at (£40) a night.

Dates
British usage: day followed by month followed by year
Written short forms: 1/6/90 = the first of June, nineteen ninety
Written longer forms: 1 June 1990, or 1st June 1990
American usage: month followed by day followed by year

Written short forms: 1/6/90 = January (the) sixth, nineteen ninety
Written longer forms: January 6 1990, or January 6th 1990
Short forms of months: Jan, Feb, Mar, Apr, Aug, Sept, Oct, Nov, Dec

Use of indirect questions

Especially when the person asked may not know the answer, it is often polite to ask
a question using an indirect form. For example, instead of:
When *will* the room *be* ready?
we might say
Do you know when the room *will be* ready? (Note the movement of *will*.)

Use of continuous forms

The use of the continuous can sometimes express greater politeness, especially with
will ('future continuous') or *would* 'conditional continuous'. It avoids suggesting
that the person is trying to do something deliberately, and suggests that the action
will take place naturally.

For example, before accepting a reservation, instead of:
How long would you stay?
We might say
How long would you *be staying*?
And after accepting a reservation, instead of:
What time will you arrive?
We might say:
What time will you *be arriving*?

Miscellaneous vocabulary

customer	face to face	reservation
double room	mind (not mind doing something)	single room
en suite	plan (v)	twin room
extra	Reception Clerk	

UNIT 7

Hotel reservations (2)
Telexes and letters

To start you off

1 Look at this telex, then try to answer the questions about it.

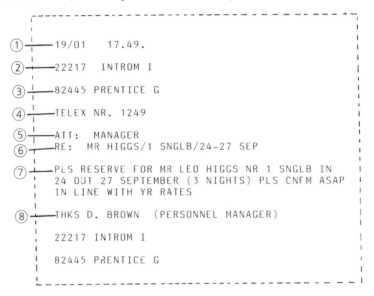

(a) Number (2) is the number and code of the *receiver*. But which numbers represent

— the number and code of the sender? _____
— the main message? _____
— the introductory reference? _____
— the ending and signature? _____
— the telex number? _____
— the attention line (the person who should deal with the message)? _____
— the date and time of the telex? _____

(b) What does the message mean? (Work this out first by yourself. Check your ideas using the list of abbreviations in the Reference Section.)

2 Look at telexes A–C below. As quickly as possible, decide which telex:

(a) is about a married couple
(b) is about a change in rooms
(c) contains a phrase meaning 'as soon as possible'
(d) suggests that the guest(s) may accept a different type of room if necessary
(e) asks when a guest will arrive
(f) is a reply to the telex in Exercise 1

A

```
12/09    11.44

22217    INTROM I

10404    LUXTRAV G

3127

PLS CHANGE RESERVATION MR/S P JONES FROM 4 NIGHTS IN
21 SEP OUT 25 SEP CP TO 3 NIGHTS IN 23 SEP OUT 26 SEP MAP.
PLS CFM ASAP.
REGDS LUXTRAV

22217 INTROM I

10404 LUXTRAV G
```

B

```
20/01    18.57

82445 PRENTICE G

22217 INTROM I

ATT:  PERSONNEL MANAGER

REYT  19/01/87 WE CNFM RESERVATION MR LEO HIGGS SNGLB IN
24 OUT 27 JAN.   RATE POUNDS 85.   PLS ADV TIME ARRIVAL.
REGDS.

82445 PRENTICE G

22217 INTROM I
```

C

```
07/10    17.35

21327    GRANHOT G

49384    CATTOURS S
TELEX NR   448

GOOD EVENING FROM CATALONIAN TOURS BARCELONA.
PLS RESERVE ROOMS FOR NBR 3 MALE LECTURERS ATTENDING
CONFERENCE LONDON IN 14 OUT 18 OCT.
SNGLB OR SNGLS PREFERRED.
CLIENTS WILL BE IN YR HTL 9.30 P.M.
THKS   ++++

21327 GRANHOT G
49384 CATTOURS S
```

3 Look at these parts of a telex replying to Telex C in the previous exercise. Put the telex in the correct order.

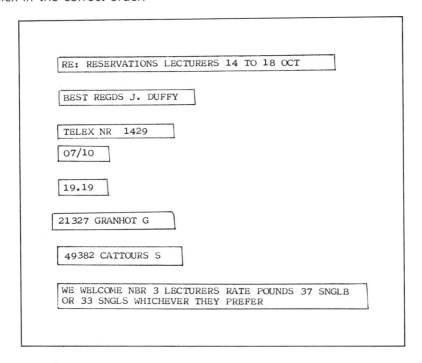

RE: RESERVATIONS LECTURERS 14 TO 18 OCT

BEST REGDS J. DUFFY

TELEX NR   1429

07/10

19.19

21327 GRANHOT G

49382 CATTOURS S

WE WELCOME NBR 3 LECTURERS RATE POUNDS 37 SNGLB OR 33 SNGLS WHICHEVER THEY PREFER

Developing the topic

4 The messages in telexes are usually abbreviated versions of the sentences we would use in everyday speech or in letters. Words may be *shortened* (see the list of abbreviations in the Language Reference section) or words may be *missed out* completely — especially words like *the, a, is, are, for, from,* etc.

Write out in full the telex messages in Exercise 2. There is more than one 'correct' answer, but the Reference Section together with the following ideas may help you:

Telex A: You could add *the, for* and change 'IN ... OUT' to 'from ... to'.
Telex B: You could add *the, for, a, is* and change 'IN ... OUT' as in Telex A. Note that in ordinary language we *advise somebody of something.*
Telex C: Not many extra words are needed, but you could add *a, the, are.* Change 'IN ... OUT' as before. Check the Language Reference section for ways of expanding the abbreviations.

5 Using the Reference Section as necessary, rewrite the following telex message by changing or abbreviating the words in italics. Omit other words completely whenever possible.

Please advise us *as soon as possible* of *your* rates for *a double room with shower* for clients *arriving on the fourteenth of June* and *departing on the seventeenth of June, Modified American Plan. Thank you.* J. Brown, Speedbird Travel Agency.

6 The Manager of the Palace Hotel has left some recorded instructions on his dicta-phone for telexes that must be sent to various people. Listen to the instructions, then:

(a)   Make a note of the message
(b)   Write the message as it would occur in a telex.

(Note: Write the message only, not the receiver's and sender's name, etc. Use phrases from the Language Reference section as necessary.)

7 Nowadays, communication by telex is more important in the hotel industry than communication by letter, especially for reservations. But a great deal of communication is still by letter, especially between the hotel and private people.

Look at the examples of how a letter is set out in the Language Reference section. Then rewrite the letter below so that the points in it come in the correct order.

(a) I look forward to hearing from you, with details of your current rates.
(b) Yours faithfully
(c) I stayed for two weeks at your hotel last summer and spent a most enjoyable holiday there.
(d) (Dr) R.J. Trees
(e) I would like to stay for another week this summer, 4th–11th July, and to reserve a room of the same type and location. Last year I stayed in a very pleasant single

47

room with bath, to the rear of the building, with a beautiful view over the golf course.

(f) Northcliffe House
Springfield
Oldshire
3 October 1989

(g) The Manager
Mountain View Inn
Oak Ridge
Upland Region

(h) Dear Sir

8 Read the section on letters in the Language Reference section. Then write a reply to the letter in Exercise 7. Choose a suitable date. Include the following points:

— Thank the client for his letter of ... (DATE OF CLIENT'S LETTER)
— Say you are very glad that the client enjoyed his stay at your hotel last year.
— Say that you can offer a single room ..., etc. (confirm details of the room, and dates, according to the request made by the client). Give suitable room rates.
— Ask the client politely to confirm the reservation, and say that you look forward to having the client with you again this summer.

ᑫᑌ

9 Letters are sometimes used to confirm in writing arrangements which have already been made in conversation.

Listen to the conversation between the Manager of a hotel and a secretary. Then complete the letter below, confirming the arrangements made in the conversation.

With reference to our conversation yesterday, I have pleasure in confirming that we are able to offer a luxury accommodation package to your clients as follows:

We shall provide ..., etc.

10 Read the extract from a letter, on the next page.

Write a suitable reply to Mr Winfield along the following lines:

— Thank the client for his letter and request (see Language Reference)
— Say that you cannot provide the accommodation the client requests for these dates (begin *Unfortunately we are unable ...*)
— Offer an alternative (e.g. a different type of room, or a room in a different part of the hotel, or the type of room requested but for different dates)

```
                                                   3rd June 1989


    Dear Sir

    I am writing to find out if it would be possible to reserve
    accommodation at your hotel for four nights, from 3rd to 7th July
    for myself, my wife and our 11 year-old daughter.  We stayed at
    the hotel some years ago in a very pleasant triple-bed room on
    the first floor, at the back of the hotel, overlooking the
    swimming pool.  We found this room very convenient and if
    possible we would like to book it again.

    Yours faithfully
    R.W. Winfield.
    (Mr) R.W.Winfield
```

Follow-up

11 Work with a partner. Compose a suitable telex or letter in reply to the situation below.

You receive this telex message:

```
CAN YOU PROVIDE NBR 150 SGLB AND CONFERENCE FACILITIES FOR
ANNUAL PAEDIATRICIANS' CONFERENCE IN 16 OUT 24 JULY? PLS CFM
ASAP.
```

You do not have enough rooms of the types requested for the dates requested. However, you do have the facilities, and you would like to stage the conference.

12 Work in groups with other students like this:

Compose (a) a telex from a travel agency to a hotel, (b) a letter from a client to a hotel. In each case request a reservation. Include information on numbers, room type and dates.

Exchange your telex and letter with those written by another group.

Now, taking part of hotel managers and reception staff, write replies to the telex and letter you received from the other group. 'Send' the telex and letter back to them.

<u>Reservations</u> (to confirm)

Letter Mr/s P Lazorio re letter 7 May – double room with bath – overlooking sea – 2nd-9th July – £45/night – includes continental breakfast.

Telex Paradise Tours – party of 20 – arriving 19 August – departing 23 August – staying twin rooms shower and toilet – bed and breakfast with dinner 19-22 August – £120 per person

<u>Reservations</u> (cannot confirm)

Letter Mr Klaus Schmidt re letter 9 May – Grande Suite unavailable 7th-13th June – Can offer Penthouse Suite – quiet, luxurious and private, all facilities, magnificent view over city – £175 per night.

Telex Darius Tours re telex 13 May – unable provide 24 single rooms with bathroom 5-10 July – Can offer 16 single £40 4 twin £25 PP PD – confirm if acceptable

13 Look at the notes on page 50 that a hotel manager has made about telexes and letters he must answer.

Write suitable telexes and letters for the manager based on the notes above. Refer to the phrases in the Language Reference section as necessary.

Language reference

Telexes

Note 1: Some useful phrases
AS REQUESTED WE HV RESERVED NBR 2 SNGLS ... (= 'As requested, we have reserved two single rooms ...')
REGRET UNABLE PROVIDE ACCOMODATION REQUESTED ... (= 'We regret that we are unable to provide the accommodation requested ...')
WE CFM YR RESERVATION ... (= 'We confirm your reservation ...')

Note 2: Common abbreviations in telexes
Below you can see some of the ways in which words may be abbreviated in telexes. *Note that it is not obligatory* to use these abbreviations. You can write the message out in full sentences, with full forms of the words if there is any possibility that the receiver will not understand.

ADV	advise	MAP	Modified American Plan
AP	American Plan		(room + 2 meals)
	(room + 3 meals)	MAR	March
APR	April	MR/S	Mr and Mrs
APPROX	approximately	NBR or NR	number
ARA	arrive/arrival	NOV	November
ASAP	as soon as possible	OCT	October
ATT/ATTN	for the attention of	PD	per day
AUG	August	PLS	please
CFM	confirm	PP	per person
CP	Continental Plan	PP PD	per person per day
	(room + breakfast)	REF	reference
DBLB	double room with bath	REYT	with reference to your telex

DBLN	double room without bath or shower	REGDS	regards
		SEP	September
DBLS	double room with shower	SGLB	single room with bath
		SGLN	single room without bath or shower
DEC	December		
DEP	depart	SGLS	single room with shower
DPT	departure	SGL(S)	single(s)
FB	full board	SUIT	double room with bath and sitting room
FEB	February		
GRP	group	TFF	tariff
HB	half board	TKS/THKS	thanks
HTL	hotel	TLX	telex
HV	have	TRP(B)	triple room (with bath)
JAN	January	TWB	twin-bedded room
JUL	July	YR	your
JUN	June	+	end of message

Letters

Study these examples of letters to and from a hotel (British layout):

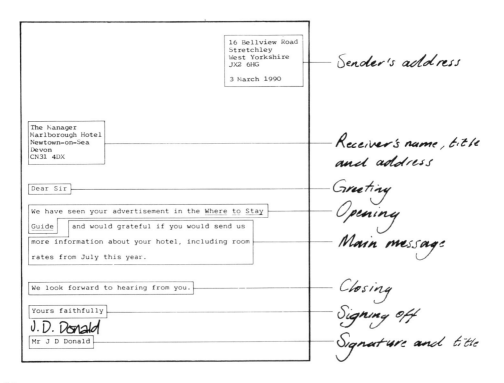

Study these phrases used in letters (British usage):

Greeting
If you know the receiver's surname: Dear Mr Smith, Dear Mrs Thomson, Dear Miss McBride, Dear Ms Fielding (if you do not know the marital status of the woman you are writing to)
If you do not know the receiver's surname: Dear Sirs (to a company or hotel), Dear Sir, Dear Madam, Dear Sir or Madam (to a person with a specific job within the company or hotel)

Opening the letter
Note: for simple requests/enquiries no special opening is needed.
(*to* the hotel)
With reference to your advertisement ..., etc.
We have read your advertisement in ... and ..., etc.
I am writing to find out if it would be possible to ..., etc.
(*from* the hotel)
Thank you for your letter of 2nd June requesting accommodation for ...
With reference to your letter of 5th May concerning ...
We have received your letter dated 27 October and enclose/have reserved ...

Main message
(*to* the hotel)
Please send ... (information, a brochure, etc)
We would like/would be grateful for ... (information, a brochure, etc.)
(*from* the hotel)
We are pleased to inform you that ...
We are glad to confirm your reservation for ...
I have pleasure in confirming your reservation for ...
As requested, we have reserved a single room with bath for ...
We enclose a brochure giving full details of ... (our rates, etc.)
We regret that we are unable to offer ...
Unfortunately, we are unable to provide ... However, we can offer ...

Closing the letter
(*to* the hotel)
Thanking you for your attention to this matter
I look forward to hearing from you
(*from* the hotel)
We would be grateful if you would confirm that this is acceptable to you
We look forward to your early confirmation
We would be most grateful if you could let us know whether this will be acceptable to you
If you need any further information, please contact us again
If you should require any further assistance, please do not hesitate to write again
We look forward to being of further assistance/serving you again in the future/welcoming you to our hotel

Signing off
(if you have used the person's name in the greeting)
Yours sincerely
(if you have used *Dear Sirs, Dear Sir, Dear Madam*)
Yours faithfully

Miscellaneous vocabulary

abbreviation
acceptance
accommodate
advise
all-inclusive
alternative
approximately
banquet
brochure
champagne
code
convenient

introductory
obligatory
package
reference
reputation
signature
special treatment
standard
telex
triple-bed room
VIP (= very important person)

Hotel records (1)
Reservations

To start you off

1 When a guest makes a reservation, the hotel makes a record of the reservation. Below, you can see some of the most important types of record

1

Day *Friday*					Date *23ʳᵈ June*		
Folio	Name	Room type	Rate	Nights	Date of booking	Remarks	Room
1	*Finch , Mr C ⎱* *Hawks, Mr M ⎰*	T.B	25	3	19/2	*Quiet*	
2	*Fontes, Mr W*	*suite*	40	4	11/3	*V.I.P*	
3	*Ortega , Mr P*	S.B	20	1	19/4	*A/c to Birds Ltd*	
4	*Smith , Mrs T.*	S.B	20	2	16/5	*+ ²⁴/₅ + ²⁵/₇ + ²¹/₈*	
5	~~*Starling Mr H*~~	~~T.B~~	~~25~~	~~3~~	~~16/5~~	~~*Cancelled 18/5*~~	
6	*Mornand ,P.*	STB 3 DB	╱	4	17/5	*Arriving 6 PM*	

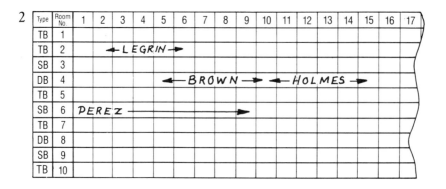

3

Name _Sparrow G_ (Mr) Arrival Date _23/6_
Mrs am/pm
Miss

Address _____ No. of nights _1_

Telephone _01 246 2648_ Ext. _123_
Single ☑ Double ☐ No. of persons _1_
Twin ☐ Suite ☐ Rate _£ 20_
Remarks _A/c to Birds Ltd_

To be confirmed Yes ☑
 No ☐ → 6 pm release?
Diary ☐ Clerk _CD_
Chart ☐ Date _19/4_

Thank you for calling

4

```
 1.1COCKERHAM/M/MR
 1 JEDSA   JEDDAH MARRIOTT        CR 1 GENR TUE 14MAR  3NTS  30000  30000
   MKT-12
 2 ARVL/GTD
CNFO-859403WQ
TRVL-91205682
PHON-N0532460221
ADRB-T/AUTOMOBILE ASSOCIATION,95 THE HEADROW,LEEDS ENGLAND,UNITED KINGDOM*LS1
%LU
INFO-ON Q 1054/06MAR/LONRC/VX

   * HISTORY *
FROM-MICK
LONRC SU VX 1554Z/06MAR
NO HISTORY
```

(a) Which of the above is:

— a standard reservation form?
— part of a reservation diary?
— part of a reservation chart?
— a display for computerized reservation?

(b) How would you use each of these records, and for what purpose?

2 Complete the paragraph below using these words:

computer, occupation, computers, received, recorded, key in, date, number, terminal, traditional, recording

Nowadays, more and more hotels use _____. As soon as the reservation is _____ it is _____ on the _____. Then later, when the Receptionist wants to know about the _____ of a room, all she has to do is _____ the room _____ and the _____ on the computer _____. However, in this unit we are going to look at other, _____ ways of _____ information which are still widely used.

3 Complete these sentences spoken by a hotel staff trainer. (You will hear them in the listening text in the next section.) Use these words:

reservation form, reservation, date, reservation diary, room, arrive, advance (×2), reservation chart, types

(a) As soon as a guest makes a _____, we write the details on the _____.
(b) Next, we can enter all reservations into a _____, under the _____ when the guests are due to _____.
(c) It's useful to know the _____ occupation of each _____, especially in hotels with many different _____ of room. So we record the _____ reservations in a _____.

Developing the topic

4 Listen to the first part of the lecture. Check your answers to Exercise 3. Stop the tape when instructed. Then listen again and answer these questions:

(a) Give two ways in which a reservation form is useful.
(b) Where do new pages go into the reservation diary? Front or back?
(c) Are names in the diary written in order of booking, or in alphabetical order?
(d) Why is the reservation chart useful when there are many different types of room?
(e) A reservation chart is also useful in hotels where guests ....
    (complete this sentence)

5 Look at the diagram. Listen to the end of the lecture. Answer these questions:

(a) What is this?
(b) What information goes on at the top of each slip?

(c) **Why is this better than a reservation diary?**
(Answer: You can arrange the _____ for each day _____, and check very quickly to see if a guest has a _____.)

RESERVATIONS

23rd June

Arr. Date 23/6	Name *Finch, Mr. C.*	Room *78*
Arr. Date 23/6	Name *Hawks, Mr. H*	Room *With Finch*
Arr. Date 23/6	Name *Jay, Mr. P*	Room *Suite*
Arr. Date 23/6	Name *Nightingale G.P.*	Room *1st 30*
Arr. Date 23/6	Name *Robin, Miss R*	Room *58*
Arr. Date 23/6	Name *Sparrow, Mr G.*	Room *58*
Arr. Date 23/6	Name *Starling*	Room *78*
Dep. Date 26/6	Account 18/5	Rate £25
Conf. Date 16/5 *Cancelled*		

Letter ☑   Telex ☐   Telephone ☐

6 Fill in the table below by putting a tick in the correct box.

	shows only one guest at a time	shows names alphabetically	shows names under date of arrival	shows each room at a glance
reservation form				
reservation diary				
reservation chart				
reservation rack				

7 Listen to the reservations on the tape. Add the details to the page from the reservation diary, below.

Day	*Monday*					Date	*8ᵗʰ July*	
Folio	Name	Room type	Rate	Nights	Date of booking		Remarks	Room
I	*Lumsden, Mr*	*single*	*30*	*6*	*29/6*			

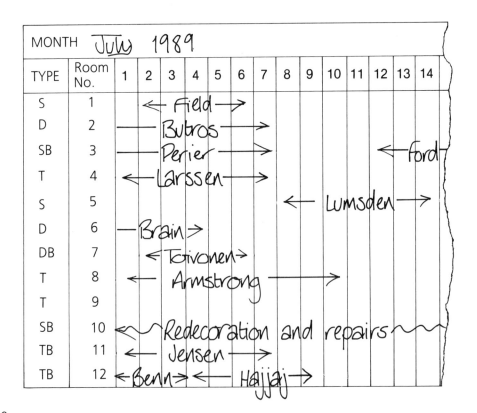

8 Listen again. Allocate each guest a room on the reservation chart below, and complete the chart.

MONTH *July* *1989*

TYPE	Room No.	1	2	3	4	5	6	7	8	9	10	11	12	13	14
S	1		*← Field →*												
D	2		*— Butros →*												
SB	3		*— Perier →*										*← ford*		
T	4		*← Larssen →*												
S	5								*← Lumsden →*						
D	6		*— Brain →*												
DB	7		*← Toivonen →*												
T	8		*← Armstrong →*												
T	9														
SB	10		*← Redecoration and repairs →*												
TB	11		*← Jensen →*												
TB	12	*← Benn →*	*← Hajjaj →*												

Look at the chart you have completed. From the table below, make sentences about the numbers of different room-types which are or aren't available *on the night of 11th July.*

The	single room(s)	is	available.
All of the	single room(s) with bath	are	occupied.
None of the	double room(s)		
One	double room(s) with bath		
Two	twin room(s)		
Three	twin room(s) with bath		

9 Here is another kind of chart used in hotels. It is called a *density chart*. If you want to know at a glance how many rooms of each type are available, it is easier to read than a reservation chart.

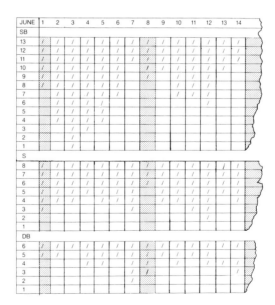

Try to make a simple density chart for the small hotel in Exercises 7 and 8 (1st–14th July). Mark in strokes for all the rooms that are reserved after Exercise 8.

Would a density chart normally be used for a hotel of this size? Why, or why not?

Follow-up

10   Point to forms and charts you have seen in this unit. Ask and answer questions like this:

Student A
What's this?

Student B
It's a reservation form
          reservation diary
          reservation rack
          reservation chart
          density chart

Student A
What does it show you?

Student B
It shows all the details of a guest's reservation
          reservations under the date of arrival
          reservations in alphabetical order
          the dates of reservations for each room
          the types of room available

11   Find out about the systems used to record advance reservations in any hotel in your area. Report to other students about how the system works.

12   Prepare a simple reservation chart (a small hotel of six rooms, for a period of fourteen days in any month you like.)

Student A
Take the part of various clients who are trying to make reservations for rooms during the 14-day period.

Student B
Tell the client if a room is available, state the price and type, and record the information in the reservation chart. If a room is not available, offer an alternative.

Continue until the hotel is fully booked. Then change round the parts of Student A and Student B, using the chart the other student prepared.

Language reference

Adverbial phrases for what forms show:
It shows one guest *at a time*

It lists the names of *guests alphabetically*
It lists the names *under date of arrival*
You can see all the names *at a glance*

Present simple used for standard procedures:
As soon as a guest *makes* a reservation we *write* the details ..., etc.
New pages *go* at the front ..., etc.

Clauses with *when* and *where:*
the date *when guests are due to arrive*
It is useful *when there are many types of room* ..., etc.
It is also useful *where guests stay a long time* ..., etc.

Vocabulary

advance (adj)
allocate
alphabetical order
chart
computer
computerized
density
density chart
diary
form
glance
key in (information in a computer)

loose-leaf
rack
record
reservation chart
reservation diary
reservation form
reservation rack
slip
standard
standardized
terminal (computer terminal)

Hotel records (2)
Check-in and after

To start you off

1   A hotel must keep a record of every guest who stays in it. Below you can see one type of record — a page from a *hotel register*.

The headings from the top of each column are missing. Fill in the headings from this list:

Family name	Full address	Room	Date
Other names	Signature	Nationality	

22/6	Sparrow	George	11 Field Lane Warrington	G. Sparrow	321	British.
23/6	Finch	Clive	27 Fowlers Walk Ealing	C. Finch	709	U.K
23/6	Finch	Janet	27 Fowlers Walk Ealing W.5	J. Finch	709	U.K

What kind of hotel will keep a record like this? What are the advantages of this kind of record? What are the disadvantages?

2   Many hotels store their information on cards called *registration cards*. Look at the registration card on the next page. Match the entries on the next page with the correct headings on the card.

(a) *J. Leblanc.* (d) *11 rue de Rivoli* (f) *Leblanc* (i) *Jean françois*
(b) *301* *Paris X1* (g) *french* (j) *29 /10/88*
(c) *Liverpool* (e) *Paris* (h) *X47302*

```
┌──────────────────────────────────────────────────────────┐
│                                                            │
│   Family name _____   Other names _____    │
│                                                            │
│   Address _____                                  │
│                                                            │
│   _____    Date _____               │
│                                                            │
│   Signature _____     Nationality _____     │
│                                                            │
│              ┌──────────────────────────┐                  │
│              │ May we book your next     │                 │
│              │ hotel — free of charge    │                 │
│              └──────────────────────────┘                  │
│                                                            │
│   Overseas visitors only:                                  │
│                                                            │
│   Passport no. _____  Place of issue _____     │
│                                                            │
│   Next destination _____                              │
│                                                            │
│   _____         ┌──────────────────┐     │
│                                    │ Room no.          │    │
└────────────────────────────────────┴──────────────────┘
```

What are the advantages and disadvantages of this type of record?

3 A reception clerk is helping a foreign guest to complete a registration form. Complete these sentences. (You will hear them in the Listening Exercise.)

(a) What's your family _____, please?
(b) How do you _____ that?
(c) And your _____ names?
(d) And your nationality? What _____ do you come from?
(e) And do you know your _____ number? Perhaps I could look at your

_____.
(f) I'm just looking for the place of _____. Ah, here we are, 'Casablanca'.
(g) And your next _____? Where are you _____ after this?
(h) That's fine, sir. Your _____ number is 252.

Developing the topic

4 Listen to the conversation between the guest and the Reception Clerk. Complete the registration form below.

Family name:	Date:	ROOM NO.
Other names:		
Nationality:		
Address:		
For overseas visitors only:		
Place of birth:		
Passport no.	Place of issue:	
Next destination:		
Signature:		

5   Ask and answer these questions with other students:

What's your family name, please?
How do you spell that?
What country do you come from?
What's your passport number?
Where was your passport issued?
Where are you going after this?

6   After guests check in, it is important to keep a record of the rooms they are occupying. In small hotels, this can be done in a *bedroom book*. You can see an example of a bedroom book, below.

Wednesday 3 May	Thursday 4 May
10 S Lodge Mr. M £20 11 SB 12 T Empson Mr/s T £35 14 TB 15 DB	10 S Lodge Mr. M £20 11 SB 12 T 14 TB 15 DB

Complete this paragraph about the bedroom book, using these words:

   arrival   registers   ten   diary   rewritten   room   page   name   stays

The bedroom book is a _____, with a _____ for each day. On each page there is a line for every _____ in the hotel. When the guest _____, the clerk writes the guest's _____ next to his room number, on the page for his _____ day. Each day the guest _____, his name is _____ on a new page. So if a guest stays for ten days, his name is written on _____ pages of the bedroom book.

7 In larger hotels a 'bed sheet' may be used. Look at the 'bed sheet' below, which is partly completed. Complete it with the information in the paragraph underneath.

Day: **Friday**   Date: **14th September**

Room	Arrivals				Staying				Departures			
	Name	Sleepers	Rate	Dep	Name	Sleepers	Rate	Dep	Name	Sleepers	Rate	Dep
101 TB					Smith Mr/s	2	£25	16/9				
102 TB									Rimmer Mr	1	£15	14/9
103 D	Stone Mr/s	2	£25	17/9								
104 TRB					Abbey Family	3	£33	15/9				
105 DB												
106 S												

Mr and Mrs Stewart and their 7-year-old daughter left Room 105 this morning. They had an extra bed in the room, and they were paying £28 a night. Mr and Mrs Stevens have just arrived, and have been allocated Room 105. They will pay £25 a night, and they will leave on 17th September. Room 106 is not available for letting, as it is being re-wired.

8 Ask and answer questions about the 'bed sheet', e.g.:

Has anyone arrived today? (Answer: Yes. Mr and Mrs Stone have arrived. They're in Room 103).
Has anyone left today?
Is anyone staying on today?
Is anyone staying in Room (103)?
Is Room (104) vacant?
Is Room (106) occupied?

9 In very large hotels the *Whitney Rack* system may be used to store information about rooms and guests. You can see a section of the Whitney Rack below, but some of the labels are missing. Listen to a lecture from a hotel staff trainer, and match the missing labels with these headings:

(a) Room numbers
(b) Arrows showing communicating rooms
(c) Room types
(d) Clear slider
(e) Red slider

(f) Yellow slider
(g) A partly filled Whitney Rack section
(h) Slips slotted into the rack
(i) Slots ready for rack slips

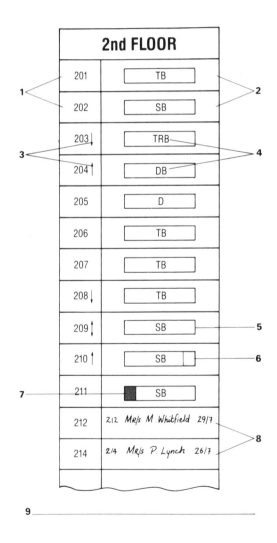

Complete the answers to these questions:

(a) What does the red slider show? The room has just been _____.
(b) What does the clear slider show? The room is _____ and _____.
(c) What does the yellow slider show? The room is _____ but not _____.

10 Put these procedures for arriving and departing guests in the correct order.

Arriving Guest

_____ (a) The room is allocated from the Whitney Rack. The slider is placed in the *red* position, to show that the room has been let.

_____ (b) The slip for the Whitney Rack is typed, and also the bill, which is given to the Cashier.

_____ (c) The guest fills in the registration card.

_____ (d) Copies of the Whitney slip are separated, with the top copy going into the Whitney Rack.

_____ (e) Copies of the Whitney slip are sent to different hotel departments.

Departing Guest

_____ (a) The guest pays the bill.

_____ (b) The slider is put in the *yellow* position, to show that the room is vacant but not ready.

_____ (c) All slips of expected departures are folded in half in the room slot (this makes it easier for the Receptionist to see expected vacancies).

_____ (d) The slip is taken out, crossed through with a coloured pen, and sent to different hotel departments.

_____ (e) The Housekeeper tells reception that the room is ready, and the slider is moved to the *clear* position.

Follow-up

11 Choose one of the following tasks:

(a) Imagine you are a hotel school teacher, training students in the Whitney System. Explain to your partner how the system works.

or

(b) Explain the advantages of changing the Whitney System to a computerized system. (You may use your own knowledge or refer to the notes at (c) below.)

or

(c) Look at the notes which a hotel trainee made below. Use the notes, and any information you have yourself, to write a short essay about the use of computers in the front office.

— nowadays many hotels use computers in front office
— information from registration card transferred to computer
— receptionist wants info about guest — enters name into computer — info about room, rate, etc. displayed immediately
— enters room numbers — names of occupants displayed
— enters dates — all arrivals/departures that date displayed
— housekeeper also access to computer terminal — enters rooms ready for occupation
— new printout of rooms and occupants every few hours — receptionist sure that room is free — reduces problems between housekeeping/reception
— computer not really new *system* — operation similar to older systems, e.g. Whitney system — but operates more quickly/efficiently
— knowledge of traditional systems still essential — taught in hotel training colleges

12 To your partner, or to the rest of your class, describe in as much detail as possible the procedures for arriving and departing guests at any hotel you know.

13 Work with two other students. For Student A's part, see below. For B and C see page 183.

Student A
The time is 10.00 am on Wednesday, 12 May. You are the Receptionist at a small hotel, with only one floor of six rooms in operation (your second floor is being redecorated). Here are your rooms:

101 T	£25	104 TB	£30
102 S	£18	105 SB	£23
103 D	£25	106 DB	£30

Rooms 101, 102 and 103 are occupied by Mr/s Stevens, Mr Barclay and Mr/s Rogers respectively, and you believe they are staying on in the hotel. Room 104 is occupied by Mr/s Wells, but as far as you know they are leaving today. One guest, Mr Reid, has just checked out of Room 105. You do not want to let Room 106, as it has just been painted, and there is a strong smell of paint.

Student B arrives at the reception desk and wants to book a room. Before you allocate the room, you telephone to the housekeeper (Student C) to find out about the state of the rooms.

(a) Act out the conversation with the guest and the Housekeeper; then speak to the guest again and say what accommodation you can offer.
(b) Write out a 'bed sheet' for the occupation of the rooms in the hotel on the *evening* of 12 May.

14 Write a 'hotel registration form' with suitable headings, ready to be filled in.

Student A
You are a reception clerk. The arriving guest (Student B) cannot read or write English, but can speak a little. Ask the guest questions and complete the registration form for him.

Student B
You are the guest. You cannot read or write English, but you can understand spoken English if it is very slow and clear, with simple words. Try to understand the receptionist's questions, and give suitable answers.

Language reference

Questions to help fill forms
What's your family name, please?
What are your other names?
How do you spell that, please?
What's your nationality?
Where do you come from?/What country are you from?
What's your passport number?
What's the place of issue? Where was the passport issued?
What's your destination?/Where are you going after this?

Use of passive to describe procedures: the room is allocated . . .; the bill is given to the cashier; etc.

Miscellaneous vocabulary

allocate	extremely	printout	signature
arrows	family name	redecorate	slot (n) and (v)
bedroom book	fold	redecoration	slider
bed sheet	issue (n) and (v)	register	slip
clear	let	registration card	terminal (computer)
communicating	nationality	respectively	ventilate
copy (n) and (v)	overseas	rewire	Whitney Rack
destination	perspex		

Using the telephone

To start you off

1 Look at the picture below. Write in these labels.

dial
handset
telephone number
extension number
telephone directory
button

2 Read these instructions from a hotel room guide.

TELEPHONE SERVICES	
Switchboard Operator	Press button at bottom right of telephone
Direct-dial outside line	0 followed by the number you wish
Reception	1
Porters	2
Housekeepers	3
Room service	4
Bar (open 11.00 am-12.00 pm	071
Restaurant (open 07.00 am-10.30 pm)	072

Now write the correct dialling instructions for these illustrations from a telephone card in the same hotel. (They are not in the same order as the guide above.) The first one is done for you.

Dial 4

3 It is a busy morning for the Switchboard Operator and Reception Clerk at the Park Hotel. Try to fill in these sentences from their telephone conversations. (There may be several 'correct' completions, but you will hear one version in the Listening exercise which follows.)

(a) The Switchboard Operator answers the phone. She says:
. . . . May I . . . .?
(b) She doesn't hear someone's name very well. She says:
I'm sorry, ..., please?
(c) She calls a guest's room, but there is no answer. She says:
I'm sorry, ...
(d) She tries to call a guest's room, but the guest is using the phone. She tells the caller: I'm sorry, the number is _____. Would you like to _____ on?
(e) A caller wants to reserve a room. The operator tells the caller: I'll _____ you through to _____.
(f) The hotel Receptionist answers the phone. He says:
. . . . May I . . . .?

Developing the topic

4 Listen to the dialogues. Check your answers to Exercise 3. Then listen again and answer these questions.

(a) What is the purpose of the calls in Dialogues 1, 2, 3 and 4?
(b) What does the Operator say when the number starts ringing in Dialogue 1?
(c) How does the caller spell her name in Dialogue 2?
(d) How does the Switchboard Operator check that she has noted the name correctly in Dialogue 2?
(e) How does the caller say her telephone number in Dialogue 3? What do you think is the nationality of the caller?
(f) How does the Operator say the telephone number in Dialogue 3?
(g) In which Dialogues did you hear the expression *put* (one person) *through* (to another person). What does it mean?

5 Study the notes about spelling names and saying telephone numbers in the Language Reference section. Then work with a partner, like this.

(a) Spell your full name and address to your partner. Your partner writes your name and address down as you spell it.
(b) Say your telephone number to your partner (and the telephone numbers of other people you know, the telephone and telex number of your hotel, etc.) Your partner writes down the numbers as you say them.

6 Work with a partner and practise conversations like this, using different names and room numbers.

STUDENT A Can I speak to Mr Baker, Room 301 please?
STUDENT B I'm sorry, he isn't in his room at the moment. Can I give him a message?
STUDENT A Yes. Please tell him Mr Lycett phoned.
STUDENT B Lycett. That's L for Lucy, Y for yellow, C for Charlie, E for Edward, double T for Tommy?
STUDENT A That's right.

7 Complete this dialogue. You can find the expressions the operator uses in the Language Reference section.

OPERATOR; Airport Hotel, good afternoon.
CALLER: Hello. This is Frank Lewis, Airport Security. . . . . the Assistant Manager, please?
OPERATOR: Just . . . . a moment and I'll put . . . . (the operator cannot connect the call immediately)
OPERATOR: Still . . . . you. (she connects the call, but there is no answer)
OPERATOR: I'm sorry, I'm not . . . . reply at the moment. Would you like to . . . .?
CALLER: No, it's OK. I'll . . . . tomorrow.

8 Write a dialogue based on the following situation. Then act out the dialogue with a partner.

Ann Cox telephones the Palace Hotel. The time is 10.00 am. The Operator at the hotel answers. Ann tells the Operator her name, saying also the name of her company, Lantern Books Ltd. She asks to speak to Mr Daniel Webb who is staying in Room 114. The Operator tries to put the call through, ringing Room 114 for some time, but there is no reply. The Operator gives this information to Ann, and offers to take a message. Ann leaves a message for Mr Webb to telephone her at 0442-231555.

9 Some hotels have special forms which they use to take messages for guests. Study the example below.

EXCELSIOR HOTEL

DATE
13 Jan

Message for ....Jake Dorricott......

Room No [204]

Caller's Name: ....Catherine Kaczmarcyk....

Telephone No: ....09-332-2977....

She cannot keep the appointment tomorrow. She will 'phone tonight at 11·00 pm about another appointment.

Message received by: ....D Fabri (Reception)....

Time: ....8·30 pm....

Who is the message from? Who is the message for? What do you think the caller said to the clerk who took the message?

10   Write messages according to the information below, as in the example.

(a) John Marsh leaving message for Mary Hopkins: 'Could you tell her I'll be waiting for her outside the theatre at 19.00?'
    John Marsh will be waiting for you outside the theatre at 19:00.

(b) Smiler's Garage leaving message for Bill Curry: 'Just tell him we've finished the work on his car.'
    . . . .

(c) Leo Weiss leaving message for Jack Stubbs: 'Please tell him my driver is coming to pick him up.'
    . . . .

(d) Maria Santos leaving message for Jaqueline Duparc: 'Tell her I'll contact her when she comes back from Paris.'
    . . . .

(e) Hassan Khayat leaving lessage for Salwa Nafisi: 'Could you tell her I've got the tickets she wanted, please?'
    . . . .

(f) Sun Travel Agency leaving message for Ron Wood: 'He should bring three passport photos to us by Monday so that we can arrange his visa.'
    . . . .

11   Look at the hotel message forms below. Listen to the callers on the tape and complete the forms correctly, writing out messages if necessary.

1.

BELLEVUE HOTEL

Message for: _____   Room no.: _____

Date: _____   Time: _____
From: _____   Tel. no.: _____

Please call at number above ☐

Will call back at _____☐

_____
_____
_____

Taken by _____

2.

👤
THISTLE HOTELS

MESSAGE FOR:

_____

ROOM No.: _____ TIME: _____

FROM:

_____
_____
_____
_____
_____
_____
_____
_____
_____
_____
_____
_____

S 01 724 (Feb 83)

TAKEN BY: _____ DATE: _____

3.

CH
CUMBERLAND
HOTEL

NAME: _____

ROOM NUMBER: _____

THE FOLLOWING MESSAGE WAS LEFT FOR YOU TODAY

BY: _____

TEL. NUMBER: _____

_____
_____
_____
_____
_____
_____

DATE: _____ TIME: _____

TAKEN BY: _____

4.

EXCELSIOR HOTEL | DATE

Message for ....

Room No [_____]

Caller's Name: ....

Telephone No: ....

Message received by: ....

Time: ....

77

12 If you are a telephone operator, what would you say in these situations? Use the words given in brackets.

(a) You promise the caller that you will make the connection with the person asked for. (put/through)
(b) You have difficulty in making the connection between the caller and the person asked for. (try/connect)
(c) You think the caller will have to wait a few moments before the connection can be made. (hold/line)
(d) There is no answer from the telephone when you ring it. (reply)
(e) You offer to tell the person what the caller wants. (message)
(f) You cannot make the connection because the person asked for is already using the telephone. You think the caller may wish to wait. (engaged/hold on)
(g) You want to know if you should ask the person to make a telephone call back to the caller. (call back)

Follow-up

13 Work with other students and act out these situations:

(a) (with one other student)
The caller wants to speak to the Assistant Manager, but the line is engaged. The caller does not want to hold. The Operator offers to ask the Assistant Manager to call back, and writes down the caller's name and telephone number.

(b) (with one other student)
The caller, Mr Leconte wants to speak to Miss Offroy in Room 201. The Operator calls the number, but there is no reply. The caller leaves a message that he will meet Miss Offrey at the usual place, tomorrow. The Operator writes down the message.

(c) (with two other students)
The Operator at the Meridian Hotel answers the phone. The caller wants to make a reservation. The Operator transfers the call to reception. The caller gives details of the type of room he/she wants, and the dates. The Reception Clerk repeats the information when he hears it, and says if a room is available.

(d) (with one other student)
You want to telephone someone in your class. The Operator calls the number, but there is no answer. Leave any message you like. (Later, the 'Operator' can read out the message.)

14 Work with two other students. Student A is the caller, Student B is the operator, and Student C is the Assistant Manager. For A's part, see below. For B and C, see page 183.

Student A

You represent a company that supplies hotel furniture. You want to speak to the Assistant Manager of the Paradise Hotel, to arrange a time when you can come and talk about your goods and your prices. You would like to arrange a meeting for the day after tomorrow. You are not free on any other day this week. The time now is 14.30.

Telephone the Paradise Hotel. Speak to the Operator and say what you want. When you get through to the Assistant Manager, try to give him all the information he asks for. Try to speak as clearly as possible, and to persuade him that he *must* see you.

Language reference

Expressions used by the operator:
When answering the phone: Good morning/afternoon, etc., NAME OF HOTEL (May I help you?);   Reception. (May I help you?) (Note: *May I help you* is optional)
On hearing who the caller wants: Hold the line, please;   I'll put you through.
When the number starts ringing: (It's) ringing for you now.
After failure to connect first time: (I'm) still trying to connect you.
If person doesn't answer: I'm sorry, there's no answer/reply;   I'm sorry, I'm not getting any answer/reply.
If the person is using the telephone: I'm sorry, the number is engaged/busy (Am.E.). Do you want to hold on?
Offering to take a message: Would you like to leave a message?;   Can I take a message?;   Can I give him a message?
Offering to arrange a return call: Shall I ask him to call you back?

Expressions used by the caller:
Can I speak to NAME, please?
Hello, is that NAME?
This is NAME.
Could you give him a message, please?
Could you ask him to phone me at TELEPHONE NUMBER?
Could you tell him I called, please?

Spelling on the phone, and phone numbers

When a letter is doubled in a name, British people usually say 'double T', 'double O', etc. Thus 'Anne' would be spelt *A — double N — E*. Similarly for numbers: 5772 would be said *five — double seven — two*. Americans would probably say the same letter or number twice.

The number 0 is usually said as 'oh' in Britain but 'zero' in America.

To clarify letters that are difficult to hear, the following systems are used:

British system

A for	Andrew
B	Benjamin
C	Charlie
D	David
E	Edward
F	Frederick
G	George
H	Harry
I	Isaac
J	Jack
K	King
L	Lucy
M	Mary
N	Nellie
O	Oliver
P	Peter
Q	Queenie
R	Robert
S	Sugar
T	Tommy
U	Uncle
V	Victory
W	William
X	Xmas
Y	Yellow
Z	Zebra

American system

A as in	Alpha
B	Bravo
C	Charlie
D	Delta
E	Echo
F	Foxtrot
G	Golf
H	Hotel
I	India
J	Juliette
K	Kilo
L	Lima
M	Mike
N	November
O	Oscar
P	Papa
Q	Quebec
R	Romeo
S	Sierra
T	Tango
U	Uniform
V	Victor
W	Whisky
X	X-ray
Y	Yankee
Z	Zulu

Some further expressions in British and American English

British English	American English
a long distance call	a trunk call
a reverse charge call (used when the person receiving the call pays)	a collect call
area code	routing number
telephone directory *or* telephone book	telephone book
Directory Enquiries	Directory Assistance
engaged	busy

Miscellaneous vocabulary

keep-fit   message   visa.

UNIT 11

Hotel services (1)
General services

To start you off

1 Think of a hotel you have worked at or visited. How would the services below be useful to a guest? How would the guest obtain these services?

(a) room service
(b) a mini bar
(c) tea and coffee (without going to the coffee shop)
(d) telephone (outside calls)
(e) telex
(f) currency exchange
(g) transport (e.g. a taxi, or transport to the airport)
(h) car parking
(i) laundry
(j) TV programmes and video films
(k) an early morning call
(l) security for valuables
(m) a doctor

2 Here are some extracts from a hotel room guide, about facilities a guest can obtain *inside the room*. Complete the extracts using the words below.

selection, 24-hour, refrigerator, local, handset, instructions, drinks, movies, dial, switchboard, alcoholic, viewed, stock, account, facility, overseas

> EARLY MORNING CALL Lift the _____ of your telephone. _____ the required time in hours and minutes using the _____ clock, eg 08.15 (8.15 am). Your phone will ring at the set time.
>
> MINI BAR Soft _____ and a selection of _____ beverages can be obtained in the _____ in your room. Items will be charged to your _____ , and the _____ replaced daily.

82

TEA AND COFFEE You will find a _____ for making tea and coffee in your room.

TELEPHONE For _____ calls, dial 0 and then the number. For long-distance or _____ calls, dial 9 to contact the_____

TV AND VIDEO programmes may be _____ on the TV set in your room. A _____ of In-house _____ is available for your enjoyment. For _____ on viewing and charges please see our separate video guide.

Developing the topic

3 Listen to the dialogues between hotel guests and an enquiries clerk. Write down the service that is being talked about in each dialogue.

Conversation 1 ....   Conversation 4 ....
Conversation 2 ....   Conversation 5 ....
Conversation 3 ....   Conversation 6 ....

4 Listen again. Answer these questions.

(a) If you are a guest, how can you make sure that nobody steals your car?
(b) How often is there transport to the airport and how long does the journey take?
(c) Where should guests leave clothes which are to be washed?
(d) What is the telex number of the hotel?
(e) If you have something valuable with you, where should you leave it?
(f) What number should you dial if you want to get something to eat in your room?
(g) Complete these sentences from the dialogues:

— You ..... your car in .... Hotel.
— Your laundry will be ..... and ..... to you by six o'clock in the evening.
— You .... a telex .... desk. We'll ....
— Jewellery .... here at reception.
— Hot and cold .... time of the day or night.

5 Look at these different ways of expressing the same idea.

mainly writing, or formal speech:	*mainly informal speech:*
Drinks can be obtained from the bar.	You can get drinks from the bar.
Car parking is available	You can park your car ....
	or There's a car park ....

Write sentences to match the sentences given. The first one is done for you.

1 (a) Soft drinks can be obtained from the mini-bar.
  (b) You can get soft drinks from the mini-bar. . . . .
2 (a) . . . .
  (b) You can get snacks from room service at any time.
3 (a) Travellers cheques can be cashed at the cashier's desk.
  (b) . . . .
4 (a) A photocopying service is available at the Business Centre.
  (b) . . . .
5 (a) Postage stamps . . . .
  (b) You can buy postage stamps at the sales desk.
6 (a) Foreign newspapers are available at the news-stand.
  (b) . . . .

6 With a partner, practise asking and answering questions from this table. If you are Student B, decide whether you want to speak formally to the guest or not. (See Language Reference section.)

Student A

How Where	can I	park my car?
		get to the airport tomorrow morning?
Can I Is it possible to		get some clothes washed?
		send a telex?
		keep some valuables in a secure place?
		get something to eat late at night?
		make tea or coffee in my room?
		get a cold drink in my room?
		make a long distance telephone call?
		see a video?
		get an early-morning wake-up call?

Student B

Reply to the guest's enquiry. Say:
(a) what the guest can do
or (b) what can be obtained, made, arranged, etc.
or (c) what facilities are available

🔲

7 Martin and Alfred have recently become Manager and Assistant Manager of a hotel in the south of England. The hotel is a little old-fashioned and they are thinking of improvements they could make, additional facilities, etc.
Listen to the conversation. Fill in the table below.

Facilities they offer now	Facilities they may offer in the future

8 In your own words, say why Martin and Alfred want to add the facilities they mention. Think of the *purposes* and *needs* that guests have. Begin like this:

They want to provide a photocopying service   *so that guests can* . . . .
for guests who need . . . .

9 Here are some more hotel services described in a hotel guide.

VALET SERVICE
SIGHTSEEING
DOCTOR
THEATRE TICKETS

HAIRDRESSING
FOREIGN EXCHANGE/TRAVELLER'S CHEQUES
PACKED LUNCHES

Match the headings above with the advice about each service below.

(a) The Hall Porter will be pleased to advise you of current shows and will make reservations to suit your requirements.
(b) For minor alterations to clothes, sewing, stain removal, etc. contact the Housekeeper.
(c) Please contact the Duty Manager if medical attention is required. Note that medical fees are the direct responsibility of hotel guests.
(d) These are available if ordered from Room Service the day prior to requirement.
(e) For tours in and around the city please contact the Hall Porter.
(f) Both of these will be exchanged at the reception desk at the displayed rate.

10 With a partner, practise giving suitable advice to guests who have the needs and purposes expressed below. In replying to the guests, you may use any of the following expressions:

You can ...
You should contact/talk to/phone to ...
... is/are available ...
... can be obtained/arranged, etc.
We can provide ...
We have ...

(a) 'I'm not feeling very well — I've forgotten to pack the pills I take for my migraine ...'
(b) 'I'd just love to get a ticket for *The Phantom of the Opera* while I'm here in London ...'
(c) 'I'll be away walking in the hills all day tomorrow, and I won't be anywhere near a restaurant ...'
(d) 'Oh dear — I've got an interview for a job tomorrow and the zip on my trousers is broken ...'
(e) 'We'd like to see something of the city while we're here ...'
(f) 'I've got no money on me at all — just one fifty dollar bill and my traveller's cheques ...'
(g) 'The baby's asleep in the room. He usually sleeps on till morning, but we're worried in case he wakes up and starts crying while we're in the restaurant ...'
(h) 'I need to contact my boss in Stockholm, urgently ...'

(i) 'I've got some papers from our sales conference here. Is there any way I can get a copy ...?'

(j) 'The embassy have told me I must supply them with three photographs tomorrow morning or they won't give me a visa ...'

Follow-up

11 Consider any of the facilities or services mentioned earlier in this unit. Tell other students in the class about any hotel you know or have worked in. Describe the *services* the hotel offers (or does not offer). Mention any services you think there *should* be or that the hotel *ought* to offer.

12 Work with a partner or a group. Write your own 'hotel guide', with an alphabetical list of the services that your hotel provides, and explanation of how they can be obtained.

Exchange the hotel guide you have written with that written by another pair or group of students.

Give the 'guide' you now have to one student in the pair or group who takes the part of an enquiries clerk. The 'clerk' uses the information in the guide to answer the queries of 'guests' (played by the partner or by other students in the group).

13 Two travelling salesmen are discussing hotels they stayed in recently. The information for one hotel is given below (Student A). The information for the other hotel is given on page 185 (Student B). Through discussion, fill in the table of services and problems for each hotel. Decide which hotel (if either) you will stay at next time.

Student A
You stayed at the Ramada Hotel. You could not get a drink sent to your room after midnight. There was a refrigerator in your room with some soft drinks, but the refrigerator wasn't working. You telephoned directly from your hotel room to your girl-friend in Ireland. You had to park your car in the street in front of the hotel, because there wasn't enough room in the car park. A guest in the room next to yours had a heart attack, and the hotel found a doctor immediately. (You can add two or three extra services and/or problems if you wish.)

RAMADA HOTEL		VICEROY HOTEL	
Service	Problems	Service	Problems

Language reference

Formal and less formal language

'Formal' language is used especially in writing, but may be used in spoken language by hotel staff, since the hotel situation is by nature fairly formal. Formal language in this unit includes:

> passive forms (Drinks can be obtained ..., etc.);
> use of *available* (A photocopying service is available ..., etc.).

Nowadays, many hotel staff would use ordinary spoken language, which is either 'informal' or 'neutral'. In this unit such language includes:

> *You can ... (get a drink from ..., do photocopying ...*, etc.)
> Use of *There's/There are* for availability: *There's a photocopier ...*, etc.

Other patterns
Discussing facilities that should be available:

We	should ought to	offer provide have	direct-dial telephones. laundry facilities. a mini-bar in every room etc.

Verbs of service provision: to *offer/provide* a service
Expressions of purpose and need
... (provide a service) so that guests can ..., etc.
... (provide a service) for guests who need ... (copies of papers, etc.)

Words for services
Baby-listening service
Baby-sitting service
Car parking
Courtesy coach
Currency exchange
Direct-dial telephoning
Doctor
Early-morning call

Miscellaneous vocabulary
access
alteration
automatically
display
embassy
foreign currency exchange
hairdressing
heart attack
install
jewellery
laundry
medical service
meter (v)
microphone
migraine
mini-bar
news-stand
outgoing (call)
packed lunches

photocopying
safe deposits
sewing
shoeshine
shoe cleaning
sightseeing
slip
stain
tea and coffee
telephone
telex
theatre tickets
transport
traveller's cheques
TV and video
valet service
valuables
zip

Hotel services (2) Directions and general enquiries

To start you off

1 Look at this *display panel* in the Wellington Hotel. What would you say if you were at the reception desk and someone asked you these questions:

(a) Where's the coffee shop?
(b) Where are the hotel shops?
(c) Where's the roof garden?
(d) Where's the disco?
(e) Where's the Manager's office?
(f) Where's room 212?
(g) Where's the Napoleon restaurant?

FLOOR 7 Napoleon Restaurant Roof Garden
FLOORS 2-6 Guests Rooms 200-640
FIRST FLOOR Guests Rooms 101-120 Waterloo Grill Manager's Office
GROUND FLOOR Reception Coffee Shop and Terrace Cafe Duke's Restaurant 1815 and Lobby Bars Hotel Shops Conference Centre
BASEMENT Beer Cellar Disco

2 Here is a *plan* of the Wellington Hotel (ground floor). Study it, and find:

— the main entrance
— the front desk
— the restaurants on the ground floor
— the shops

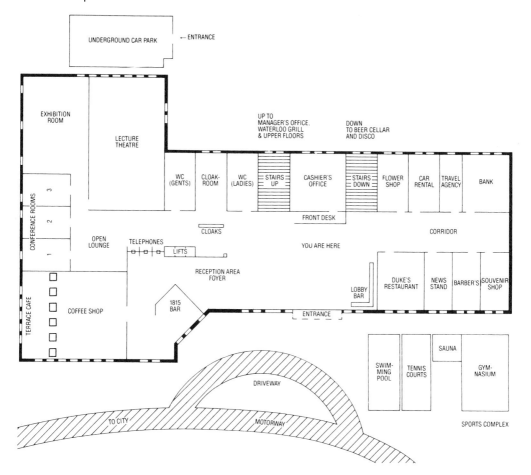

Match the enquiries about *where things are* (1—7) below with the *replies* (a)—(g) which follow. Use the plan above if necessary. Make sure you can find each place mentioned, on the plan.

1. I'm looking for the news-stand
2. Where's the nearest bar, please?
3. Can you tell me where the Cashier's office is, please?
4. Where can I change my traveller's cheques?
5. Where can I get a meal at this time of night?
6. Could you direct me to the car park, please?
7. I'm trying to find the Duke's Restaurant.

(a) This is his office, right behind us — the office through this door here.

(b) The bank will be able to help you, I think — it's along that corridor, on the left.

(c) The coffee shop is open 24 hours a day — over there, to the right of the 1815 Bar.

(d) The entrance is behind the hotel. There's an attendant who will park the car for you, if you give him your keys.

(e) There's one right behind you, or you can get a drink in the 1815 Bar, next to the coffee shop.

(f) It's the shop along there on the right, next to the Duke's Restaurant.

(g) It's on the top floor, but I'm afraid it's closed now. The Waterloo Grill on the first floor is still open, or you can get a meal in the coffee shop, over there.

3 Match each *general enquiry* below (1—4) with a *reply* (a)—(d).

1. Is there any dancing in the hotel?

2. Is it possible to book a sauna?

3. We'd like to buy some souvenirs.

4. Can we leave our coats somewhere?

(a) The cloakroom is along there on the right.

(b) You'll find some nice ones in the shop along the end of that corridor, on the right.

(c) Yes. We have a disco down at the bottom of these stairs. It starts at ten o'clock.

(d) Yes. If you go back outside through the main entrance there you can book the one in our sports complex.

Using the plan as necessary, complete the enquiries about where things are, and the replies, below. You will hear them on the tape.

(a) How can I _____ to the Terrace Cafe please?
    It's on _____ floor. Go _____ through the coffee shop, and you'll _____ it just in _____ of you.
(b) Could you possibly _____ me to the tennis courts, please?
    If you go _____ through the main door you'll see them on the left _____ you go out.
(c) We're _____ for the bar.
    The lobby bar is just _____ there, _____ you madam.
(d) Is this the right _____ for the souvenir shop?
    Just go along to the _____ of the _____. You'll see it _____ the bank.
(e) Can you _____ me the _____ to the disco please?
    Yes. Just go _____ these stairs and follow the corridor along to your right.

Developing the topic

4 Listen to enquiries 1–5. Check your answers to Exercise 3. Then answer these questions:

(a) At which end of the coffee shop is the Terrace Cafe?
(b) What are the tennis courts part of? What are they next to?
(c) What other bar does the clerk mention? Where is it?
(d) According to the clerk, the souvenir shop is the _____ shop on the right, and it is _____ the barber's.
(e) How will the guest recognize the disco? What does the clerk say?

5 Look again at the plan of the Wellington Hotel. Complete the enquiries below with these words:

the conference rooms, the lecture theatre, Mr Johnson, the Manager, a public payphone, a taxi

(a) A: Excuse me. I'm trying to find ....
    B: They're all facing the open lounge. Along to your left, and straight on, past the lifts.

(b) A: Which way are ....?
    B: Along there to your left, madam. Past the cloakroom and the ladies' room, next to the lifts.

(c) A: Can you tell me where I'll find ....? I have an appointment.
    B: Upstairs, on the first floor, sir. I'll just give a ring to make sure he's there.

(d) A: Where can I get ....?
    B: They're on your right as you go outside the main entrance. The Hall Porter will find one for you.

(e) A: Excuse me. Am I going the right way for ....?
    B: Yes. Through the open lounge and then turn right. It's next to the conference rooms.

Work with a partner. Practise enquiring about and giving directions to *the conference rooms, a telephone, the Manager's office, a taxi, the lecture theatre.* Try do do this without looking at the dialogues above, but use the plan on page 91 as necessary.

6 Complete the directions below which were given by staff *in various parts* of the Wellington Hotel. Use these expressions. Each expression should be used only once.

straight ahead	in front of you	along	on your left
follow the sign	turn left	these stairs	opposite
can't miss it	come to	outside	through	as you leave

(a) Go .... and you'll find the conference rooms right ....
(b) The exhibition room? Go .... the corridor and then ....
(c) Just .... to the beer cellar and you'll .... the disco.
(d) Ah yes, the sports complex. Go .... the hotel, ... the main entrance. You'll see it .... the hotel, ...
(e) Go up ...., to the first floor. You'll see his office .... the Waterloo Grill.

7 Imagine you are standing near the reception desk. Ask and answer questions about any place on the hotel plan, like this:

Student A
Where's ...?
I'm looking for ...
Can you tell me the way to ...?
Can you tell me where ... is?
Can you tell me where I'll find ...?
Could you direct me to ...?
Am I going the right way for ...?

Student B
It's on this floor/in the basement/over there/next to .../on your right as you go out, etc.
(Go) along the corridor/downstairs/through the lounge/to your left, etc. You'll see it just in front of you, etc.

8 Directions about how to find a room or service are important. But other kinds of information are important also. When a guest enquires about a service, etc., we may have to mention:

— how to find a place
or
— the person in the hotel staff who should be contacted
or
— where to look for information (in a booklet, brochure, poster, etc.)
or
— general information (about prices, opening hours, etc.)

Read the dialogues below.

(1)
GUEST: Is it possible to get a taxi from the hotel to the airport after midnight?
CLERK: Certainly sir. If you speak to the Hall Porter he'll call one for you at any time. The fare is around £15 after midnight.

(2)
GUEST: Can you tell me what videos they're showing on the hotel TV tonight?
CLERK: Tonight there's the latest Bond film followed by *Jaws 5*. You'll find a complete list for the month in the brochure on top of your TV set.

(3)
GUEST: I've heard you have a good gymnasium in the hotel. Would it be possible to use it?
CLERK: Certainly sir. It's in our sports complex, on your left as you go out through the main entrance. It has some first-class equipment, and a sauna attached to it.

(4)
GUEST: Is there anywhere here I can get a copy of the *New York Times?*
CLERK: Try the news-stand, along the corridor, on the right. It has a good selection of foreign newspapers and magazines.

From the dialogues above, find examples of:

— directions for how to find something
— a person in the hotel who should be contacted
— where to look for information
— general information

9 Listen to the enquiries on the tape. Stop the tape when instructed. Write what each enquiry is about.

Enquiry 1 ....   Enquiry 5 ....
Enquiry 2 ....   Enquiry 6 ....
Enquiry 3 ....   Enquiry 7 ....
Enquiry 4 ....   Enquiry 8 ....

10 Listen again to the enquiries. As you listen, look at the *outline* of the reply that the clerk gives in each case.

1. give keys to Hall Porter — over there by door — will arrange for you — charge £3
2. different show every night — tonight Layla's belly dancers — poster on hotel notice board — details of all shows next two weeks
3. souvenir shop along corridor on right — selection of souvenirs from this part of the world — open till eight o'clock
4. Waterloo Grill — first floor — closes midnight
5. no problem — have telephone directories for most areas — I — get directory for Birmingham
6. travel agency — second from end of corridor — makes bookings for all big shows — open tomorrow nine o'clock
7. around 5.30 most days — late-night shopping till 8 Friday nights
8. ordinary car park behind hotel — free — or lock-up underground car park — charge £5/night

Work out a complete version of each reply to each enquiry

11 Listen again. This time you will hear each enquiry followed immediately by its reply.

Compare the replies on the tape with the replies you worked out for Exercise 10. (Do not expect them to be the same word for word.)

Now, without looking at your book, try to act out with your partner enquiries similar to those in Exercises 8–11. You can use the original words and ideas, or your own words or ideas.

Follow-up

12 Tell other students about the layout of any hotel you know. Mention any interesting points about the location of restaurants, bars, recreation facilities etc.

13 With another student, make enquiries about services and reply to these enquiries. You can refer to the plan of the Wellington Hotel on page 91, or to the plan of any hotel you know. When replying:

— say where things are, *or*
— mention members of the hotel staff who can help, *or*
— say where to look for information, *or*
— give general information.

14 Work with a partner. For Student A's part see below. For Student B's part see page 185.

Student A
You are a guest in a hotel (not the Wellington Hotel). You want to find out about the following:

— about entertainment in the hotel
— about a suitable restaurant in the hotel to entertain the Manager of your company
— about booking a tennis court
— about changing a flight reservation
— about finding a brown leather briefcase which you think you lost in the hotel

Make enquiries of Student B. Be ready to give more details if Student B needs them. Ask for directions if necessary.

Language reference

Enquiring about where things are
Where's ...?
I'm looking for/trying to find ...
Can you tell me the way to ...
Can you tell me where ... is?/Can you tell me where I'll find ...?
Could you direct me to ...?
Am I going the right way for ...?
How can I get to ...?
Which way is ...?

Giving directions
(a) (location)
It's on (the first floor, etc.)/in (the basement)/over there/beside .../next to .../
opposite .../on your left (as you go out, etc.). Etc.
(b) (movement)
Go along .../through .../left/to your left/downstairs .../straight ahead. Etc.
Turn right (at the end of the corridor, etc.)
Follow the sign to ...
(c) (recognition)
You'll see it (right in front of you, etc.)
You can't miss it

General enquiries and requests
Is it possible to .../Would it be possible to ...?
Is there anywhere I can (get a meal, etc.)?
Can I get (a meal/my car washed, etc.)?
Do you have ...?/Have you got ...?
I'd like to get ...
Can you tell me about ...?
Can you tell me ... (what time ..., etc.)?

Replies to general enquiries and requests
Yes, there's a ...
Certainly, sir. You can ...
Yes, we have ...
(+ directions, advice about member of staff to contact, advice about where to get
further information, etc.)

Miscellaneous vocabulary

attached
attendant
auditorium
beer cellar
Bingo
booklet
briefcase
brochure
cabaret act
copy
corridor
directions
downstairs
enquiry
entertainment
equipment
fare

first-class
flight
floor show
gents
gymnasium
ladies
late-night shopping
leather
lecture theatre
light (snack, etc.)
lobby
lock-up (car park)
lost property
lottery
lounge
magician

membership
network
notice board
payphone
poster
property
public
sauna (bath)
secure
souvenir
sports complex
steak
telephone directory
temporary
tennis court
upstairs

Hotel services (3)
The hotel as a product

To start you off

1 A hotel is a *product* and hotel staff should be able to *sell* the product — to talk about the hotel, rooms, facilities, etc., so that guests want to stay in the hotel and use its facilities.

With two or three other students, think of *selling points* in hotels that you have visited or worked in. Make a list, then report items on the list to the rest of your class.

2 If you want to sell a product, you must know the product very well. But what are the most important things to know?

With two or three other students, put these points in order of importance.

(a) Public areas (knowing about lounges, reading rooms, toilets, etc.)
(b) Food and eating facilities (knowing about restaurants and bars, when they are open, and what they serve, etc.)
(c) Rooms (knowing individual rooms, their location, equipment and facilities)
(d) People (knowing the people in charge of different departments of the hotel)
(e) The hotel (knowing room rates, management, full postal address, transport connections etc.)
(f) General facilities (knowing about laundry, car hire, hotel shops, sports facilities, etc.)
(g) Rules (knowing rules about payment, checkout times, last orders, etc.)
(h) The competition (knowing what other hotels in the same area offer)
(i) Location and environment (knowing about the resort where the hotel is situated, its facilities and areas of interest nearby)

3 Complete these sentences from a lecture given by a staff trainer.

(a) You should be able to give the full postal _____ of the hotel, together with the telephone _____ and the telex _____.

(b) You should know the owner of the hotel, and the General _____.

(c) Obviously, you have to know the types of _____, and the _____ for each type of room.

(d) You ought to know the transport connections for the hotel — how to get to it by road, by bus or by _____.

(e) And you should know where guests can _____ their cars.

(f) And you should know if the hotel is mentioned in any _____ books.

(g) You should know about any _____ that have to be followed — restrictions about payment, etc.

Developing the topic

| ⌂⌂ |

4 Listen to the lecture given by the staff trainer. Check your answers to Exercise 3.

Then read the fact sheet that the staff trainer talks about, below. Some of the words have been deleted and replaced by dotted lines. Listen to the lecture again, and work out what the words are (numbered 1–10).

Hotel name: *Royal George Hotel*

① .... *204 Blackwood Road, Fenton, Newshire NW2.3UY.*

② .... *(0556) 613989*   Telex: *82444*

③ .... *Trustee Hotels PLC*   General manager: *A.W. Cowle*

Rooms ④ ....

Singles	*£40 - £48*	Check-in: *22·00*
Twins	*£72 - £88*	
Doubles	*" "*	⑤ .... *09·30*
Suites	*£120 - £140*	

⑥ ....   ⑦ .... *Car park behind hotel*
Free Lock-up garage £5 per night.

Road: *A74 from Brentford, then B1720*
Bus: *Green Bus 214 from Brentford*
⑧ .... *Brentford Station (main line Cheston – Redwich)*

⑨ .... *Hutton's Hotel & Restaurant Guide*

Star rating   AA ✱✱✱✱   RAC ✱✱✱

⑩ .... *Proof of identity or prepayment necessary for chance bookings after 21·00*

5 Write out a sheet with headings like those in Exercise 4. Fill in as much information as you can for *any* hotel (within a given city or geographical area). If there is anything you don't know now, try to find out the information later. Hotel brochures may help you.

With other students, compare hotels according to the information written on the fact sheet.

Decide whether it would be possible for any of the hotels to form a group so that, if one hotel is full, the Receptionist could recommend another, similar hotel.

6 To make sure that you know the most important things about a room you can use a check-list of points. Look at the check-list of points on the left below. Match them with the information for Rooms 100—110 of the Grand Hotel, on the right below.

ROOM CHECK-LIST

1. Location in hotel: *telephone at desk, radio built into bed, colour T.V.*

2. Number of beds and size: *Lift number 1- nearest to reception desk.*

3. Furniture and fittings: *overlooks front gardens.*

4. Bathroom/shower/toilet? *lift and lift controls suitable for guests using wheel-chairs*

5. Power points: location and rating: *light pinewood, modern Scandinavian.*

6. Furnishings style & room decor: *quiet (windows double-glazed)*

7. Telephone, radio, television? *heating and A/C control panel next to main door*

8. Heating and air conditioning? *first floor, front*

9. View from window: *3 power points (next to main door, bathroom door, and desk)*

10. Noise levels: *twin beds, 6×4 metres*

11. Access for handicapped?

bathroom with shower attachment, toilet

12. Nearest lift:

2 armchairs, writing desk, built-in Wardrobe, 2 bedside tables, 1 coffee table, luggage rack standard lamp, desk lamp.

7 Now make a check-list for yourself, copying out the words on the left above. Try to complete as much of it as you can for any hotel room you know.

8 Listen to the four extracts in which a hotel employee is talking. In which extract does the hotel employee talk about:

— the hotel in general?
— the rooms?
— places to eat in the hotel?
— other facilities?

9 Listen again and complete these sentences from the dialogues.

(a) The .... sir, if you .... meal. Or
....................., or from Room Service ....
(b) The hotel is .... over Clearwater Lake.
(c) Yes certainly madam. You can use .... at any time.
Or perhaps you .... our new Sports
Complex? They include .... swimming pool, and
....
(d) We can give you .... for $75 a night, or
.... and has cable television for $90 a night.

10 Whenever possible, hotel staff should:

(a) use *descriptive phrases* when talking about the hotel and facilities
(b) Offer an *alternative* when saying what is available
(c) try to interest guests in *something 'better'* than what they have in mind
(d) suggest *facilities* which guests may find useful

From the sentences in Exercise 9, find examples of ways in which the hotel employee does each of these things.

11 Here are some sentences which a hotel employee might use when speaking to guests, but the words are in the wrong order. Write them out correctly.

(a) *to a guest who is looking at the 'set' dinner menu:*
> prefer/you'd/Perhaps/à la carte/our/menu/specialities/has/which/some/house/the/of.

(b) *to a guest who is picking up his key late in the evening:*
> is/bar/still/open/the/you'd/like/if/drink/a/The/up/go/before/to/you/your/room.

(c) *to a guest who is making a reservation:*
> comfortable/very/room/It's/fine/view/the/hills/of/a/with/a.

(d) *to a family who are making a reservation:*
> offer/We/can/triple/room/a/we/can/or/you/give/double/a/room/extra/an/bed/with

(e) *to a guest who is reserving a room for five days:* (two sentences)
> week/you/Would/like/stay/a/full/for/madam/to?
> you/offer/can/We/rate/special/all-inclusive/rate/a.

(f) *to a businessman who asks to borrow a typewriter:* (two sentences)
> interested/you/be/in/Would/our/service/secretarial?
> reasonable/rates/Our/very/are.

(g) *to a guest who is asking about another hotel in the same chain:* (two sentences)
> marvellous/decor/style/the/in/an/palace/Arabian/of/has/sultan's/It.
> furniture/fittings/and/The/hand-made/are.

Look again at the sentences you have written. Say which sentences:

(a) contain descriptive phrases
(b) offer alternatives
(c) try to interest guests in something 'better'
(d) suggest facilities which guests may want to use

Follow-up

12 If you work in a hotel you should also be able to recommend the *restaurants* in the hotel. Even if you do not work in the restaurants you should be able to give information about them. Here is a restaurant check-list.

Location in hotel _____
Opening times _____
Last orders _____
Licensed to sell alcohol? _____
Rules about dress? _____

Minimum charge? _____
Service charge _____
Credit cards _____
Decor/style/theme _____
Special features _____
Menu details/specialities _____
Charge to room? _____
Name of Restaurant Manager _____
Booking necessary? _____

Fill in this check-list for any hotel restaurant you know.

13 Here are some typical advertisements in tourist guidebooks. They mention some selling points of hotels.

1

 "WELCOME TO THE HÔTEL GEORGE V!"

The world's discerning travellers have enjoyed VIP treatment at the George V ever since that day in 1928 when the doors opened for the first time.

Sixty years on: the same impeccable service and palatial accommodation is enjoyed by discerning convention groups and deserving incentive achievers.

Organisers often wonder how even such a vastly experienced hotel can give personal attention to hundreds of delegates . . .

simple — supremely professional staff in every department.

— the largest deluxe capacity in Paris.
— 351 elegantly furnished rooms and suites.

— Twenty-one beautifully-equipped meeting rooms including an opulently appointed ballroom: conventions for 600 are accommodated as readily as a boardroom summit for ten

and — the rest is a George V secret!

Even today the George V provides welcome sanctuary from the bustle of Paris. Yet it stands just off the Champs Elysees in the centre of the business and haute couture district.

perfect location — perfect peace — perfect conventions

Hotel George V, 31 Avenue George V, 75008 PARIS, FRANCE. Telephone: 1-47 23 54 00 Telex: 650082
UK Regional Sales Office Telephone: 01-759-3524 Telex: 948 121 Fax: (0753) 693105

4

**ALL MANNER OF CONFERENCES
AT THE KING'S MANOR**

**FAMILY OWNED AND MANAGED
70 BEDROOM HOTEL**

Situated 4 miles east of Edinburgh City Centre

* 4 Function/Conference Suites for 10 up to 120 persons
* 7 Additional Seminar areas available
* Comprehensive catering arrangements
* 2 Bars
* All bedrooms with private facilities, colour TV, telephone, radio, hair dryer and tea/coffee maker
* Bedroom with four poster available
* Large car park

— E D I N B U R G H — —

100 Milton Road, East, Edinburgh EH15 2NP
Telephone: 031-669 0444
Telex: 727237

Can you find any examples of these points from the advertisements?

	(Hotel 1)	(Hotel 2)	(Hotel 3)	(Hotel 4)
TYPE				
LOCATION				
DECOR				
LEVEL OF COMFORT				
FACILITIES				
SERVICE				
CUISINE/RESTAURANTS				

Now work with a partner. Act out a conversation between a member of staff at one of the hotels, and a customer who is interested in staying there, and who is making enquiries.

Language reference

Expressions of advice: You should know,   You should be able to ...;   You ought to ...;   You have to ...;   You must ....

Ways of describing facilities: *with* a bath;   *is* centrally-heated;   *has* a fine view ....

Giving alternatives: We have X (+ description) *or* Y (+ description)

Making suggestions: Perhaps you'd like to ...;   It's still open, if you'd like to ...;   Would you like ...?;   Would you be interested in ...?

Vocabulary of hotel and description of facilities
fittings
dress
decor (= the general style in which an interior is decorated and furnished)
theme
access
last orders
licensed
power point
rating (star rating; power rating)
restriction
location
AA (= Automobile Association)
RAC (= Royal Automobile Club)
à la carte

Miscellaneous vocabulary
cable television
handicapped
hand-made
marvellous
sultan

Check-out

To start you off

1 (a) What happens at check-out? Complete the sentences below:

The guest hands over his key, and says that he wants to _____ out.

The cashier checks to see if there are any _____ that have still to be added to the _____. He makes up the complete bill, and _____ it to the Reception Clerk, who gives it to the _____. The Reception Clerk answers any _____ about the bill which the guest wishes to ask.

The guest _____ the bill, and is given a _____. Then the Clerk marks the _____ as 'vacant but not ready', and notifies the other _____ of the hotel (housekeeping, telephones, etc.) so that they can update their lists.

(b) What are the main ways in which a guest can pay a bill? Unscramble the letters below to find out:

> QUEECH _____
> SHAC _ _____
> DITCER DRAC _____ _____

And a guest who comes from another country may want to change:

> ROFGEIN RURCCENY _____ _____

or to cash a:

> VARTLEELRS' CQUEHE _____ _____

2 You may have to take certain precautions when payment is made. Write in the methods of payment to which the precautions below apply. Sometimes there is more than one answer.

(a) Check the expiry date. ....
(b) Write the number of the cheque guarantee card on the back ....
(c) Compare signatures ....

(d) **Run a number through a computer, or check it against a list**
. . . .

(e) **Look at it carefully and hold it up to the light** . . . .

(f) **Telephone the guest's bank** . . . .

(g) **Compare it with pictures in a book** . . . .

3 Complete these sentences spoken by a clerk to a guest on check-out. You will hear the sentences on the tape.

(a) (when the guest asks to check out) Certainly sir, I'll get you your _____.

(b) How would you like to _____ sir? Credit card?

(c) I'm sorry sir, but I'm _____ this credit card has _____.

(d) I'm afraid we wouldn't normally accept a _____ without a valid cheque _____ card.

(e) If you'd like to wait a moment, we'll put a telephone call through to your _____.

Developing the topic

4 Listen to the dialogue. Check your answers to Exercise 3. Then listen again and answer these questions.

(a) How does the guest want to pay at first?

(b) Why is this not possible?

(c) How does the guest want to pay next? What difficulty is there?

(d) How does the clerk offer to solve the problem?

(e) What does the guest remember at the end of the dialogue?

(f) Two companies which issue cards are mentioned in the dialogue. What are their names?

(g) What other kinds of credit or charge card do you know about?

5 Match the phrases on the left with the situations on the right.

PHRASE	SITUATION
Can I check out now, please?	The clerk wants to see the guest's credit or cheque card.
I'll get you your bill from the cashier.	The clerk expresses the goodwill of the hotel.
Are you paying by credit card, sir?	The clerk points out that the credit or cheque card is no longer valid.

Do you take American Express here?	The clerk accepts payment and gives a receipt.
Do you have your card, sir?	The clerk wants to know about the method of payment.
I'm sorry sir. This card seems to be out of date. Do you have another card?	The guest wants to know if a certain card is acceptable.
That's fine sir. Here's your receipt.	The customer wants to pay the bill and leave.
We hope you've enjoyed staying with us.	The clerk promises to get the guest's bill.

6 Practise with a partner using ideas or phrases from the tables below. You can add additional comments and complete the conversation in any suitable way.

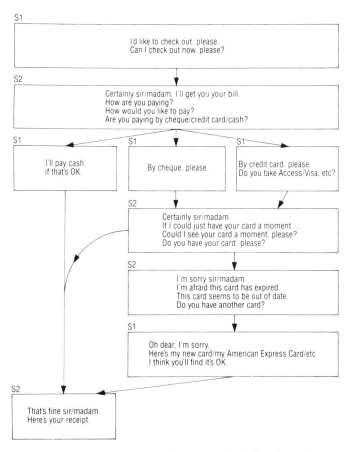

S1

> I'd like to check out, please.
> Can I check out now, please?

S2

> Certainly sir/madam. I'll get you your bill.
> How are you paying?
> How would you like to pay?
> Are you paying by cheque/credit card/cash?

S1

> I'll pay cash, if that's OK.

S1

> By cheque, please.

S1

> By credit card, please.
> Do you take Access/Visa, etc?

S2

> Certainly sir/madam.
> If I could just have your card a moment . . .
> Could I see your card a moment, please?
> Do you have your card, please?

S2

> I'm sorry sir/madam.
> I'm afraid this card has expired.
> This card seems to be out of date.
> Do you have another card?

S1

> Oh dear, I'm sorry.
> Here's my new card/my American Express Card/etc.
> I think you'll find it's OK.

S2

> That's fine sir/madam.
> Here's your receipt.

(End the conversation in a polite way with expressions of goodwill, goodbyes, etc).

111

7 Look at the headings below for the kinds of things that go on a guest's bill. Covering up the explanations below, can you explain these headings in your own words, with examples?

ACCOMMODATION   FOOD   DRINK   VALUE ADDED TAX
SUNDRY SALES   DISBURSEMENTS   SERVICE CHARGES

Now match the headings above with the explanations below:

_____ This includes breakfast, lunch, afternoon tea, drinks other than alcohol or minerals (e.g. tea, coffee), and other light refreshments. It may be served in the restaurant, the lounge, or the guest's bedroom.

_____ These include charges a guest may have to pay for such items as telephone calls, laundry, car hire, garage, hairdressing, newspapers.

_____ This is the basic charge for all guests who stay at least one night. Depending on the plan followed, it may also include breakfast, or other meals.

_____ These are payments the hotel may make on behalf of a guest, for example for taxis, theatre tickets, or repairs to guest's belongings.

_____ In the UK and some other countries, this is a tax which must be added to all services in the hotel except 'disbursements'. Many hotels include this tax in the rates they quote, but others add the tax on after the rest of the bill is added up.

_____ This includes all alcoholic drinks and minerals ('soft drinks'). They may be served in the bar, restaurant, or in guests' rooms.

_____ This is a percentage that some hotels add to the bill for all services provided. It replaces 'tips' to individual employees.

8 Look at this example of a hand-written bill. It does not use all the headings above, but it includes the same types of item. Answer these questions:

(a) Which items on the bill refer to accommodation, food, drink, sundry sales, disbursements, service charge?
(b) Do the charges include Value Added Tax?
(c) What do 'carried forward' and 'brought forward' mean? Carried forward to what? Brought forward from what?

112

REGENCY HOTEL
Newtown

Name .. Mr. J. Peters .... Apartment No .. 6 ......

199-	July 12		July 13		July 14		
Brought forward			35	25	73	20	
Apartments	25	50	25	50			
Early morning tea			0	45			
Breakfast			2	25	2	25	
Luncheon					4	50	
Afternoon tea							
Dinner	4	80	5	40			
Other food							
Liquor	3	45	2	25	1	80	
			1	80	1	35	
Sundry sales	0	60			0	99	
Paid outs	0	90	0	30	3	00	
					87	09	
Service 10%					8	73	
Carried forward	35	25	73	20	95	82	

9 Here is an example of a mechanized hotel bill. Read it and answer the questions below.

	Room No 345		Welcombe Hotel Bournehampton, Wessex				

	Name		J. Blank, Esq.				

REMARKS		DATE	DETAILS		CHARGES	CREDITS	BALANCE DUE	ROOM NO
	1	-2-4-8-	FLOOR	MEAL	' 21.00			
	2	-2-4-8-	FLOOR	DRNK	'10.00			
	3	-2-4-8-	FLOOR	CIGR	' 2.00		' 33.00	
	4	-2-4-8-	—— DISBT	TLGM	' 1.00			
	5	-2-4-8-	PHONE	——	' 0.25		' 34.25	
	6	-2-4-8-	FLOOR	(-)DRNK		' 3.00		
	7	-2-4-8-	FLOOR	DRNK	' 5.00		' 36.25	
	8	-2-4-8-	APART	——	'30.00			
	9	-2-4-8-	MISC	——	'10.50		' 70.75	
	10	-3-4-8-	FLOOR	MEAL	' 7.68			
	11	-3-4-8-	—— NEWS	——	' 0.30			
	12	-3-4-8-	REST	MEAL	'11.60		' 96.33	
	13	-3-4-8-	—— TAILR	——	' 1.75		' 98.08	
	14	-3-4-8-	GRILL	MEAL	'10.40			
	15	-3-4-8-	SURCH	SERV	' 0.65			
	16	-3-4-8-	LNGE	DRNK	' 0.70		'109.83	
	17	-3-4-8-	—— ADJST	CIGR		' 1.25	'108.58	
	18	-3-4-8-	MISC	AUTO	' 9.70			
	19	-3-4-8-	—— DISBT	THEA	' 5.40		'123.68	
	20	-3-4-8-	APART	——	'30.00			
	21	-3-4-8-	MISC	——	' 2.38		'156.06	
	22	-4-4-8-	FLOOR	MEAL	' 2.14			
	23	-4-4-8-	—— NEWS	——	' 0.30			
	24	-4-4-8-	REST	MEAL	' 5.75		'164.25	
	25	-4-4-8-	—— LNDRY	——	' 2.35			
	26	-4-4-8-	SURCH	——	'15.14		'181.74	
	27	-4-4-8-	—— CASH	——		'100.00	' 81.74	
	28							
	29							
	30							
	31							

ACCOUNTS DEPT

(a) What was the accommodation charge per night?
(b) How much was the charge for use of the telephone? laundry? newspapers?
(c) What disbursement did the hotel make on behalf of the guest? What do you think it was for?
(d) Where can you find a charge for food? Where can you find a charge for drinks?
(e) The guest paid some money to the hotel during his stay. How much did he pay? In which column can you see this?
(f) How much does the guest owe the hotel?

10 Look at the abbreviations used in bills. Write in what they mean, using the headings below.

ADJST	. . . .	NEWS	. . . .
APAR	. . . .	NGHT	. . . .
AUTO	. . . .	PHONE	. . . .
CHEM	. . . .	REST	. . . .
CIGS	. . . .	SERV	. . . .
DISBT	. . . .	SURCH	. . . .
DRINKS	. . . .	TAILR	. . . .
FRUT	. . . .	THEA	. . . .
LNDRY	. . . .	TLGM	. . . .
LNGE	. . . .		

Restaurant   Bookstall/news-stand   Chemist/drug store
Telephone   Laundry   Disbursement   Accommodation
Theatre tickets   Car hire or garage   Night waiter
Valet and dry cleaning   Fruit/flower shop
Telegram or cables   Surcharge   Lounge
Service charge   Cigarettes   Drinks
Adjustment or allowance

11 Sometimes bills explain charges through the use of *code letters*. Look at the bill below. The explanation of *some* of the code letters and charges has been badly printed, and a guest is puzzled about the bill.

Listen to the dialogue as often as necessary, and fill in the explanations for the code letters.

MERCURY HOTEL					BIRMINGHAM W.1			

TELEPHONE (021) 921 6973		Room No	Name		Date	Rate
TELEX MERCURY BIRMINGHAM		462	S. Randall		21.4.90	£28
					Duration	

	DATE	DETAILS		ROOM No	CHARGES	CREDITS	BALANCE
	APR 21	APART.		462	28.00		
	APR 21	⋯	J	462	8.50		36.50
EXPLANATION OF CODES	APR 22	REST'R	D	462	4.50		41.00
	APR 22	SVCE	L	462	7.00		48.00
D – ⋯	APR 22	REST'R	E	462	8.75		56.75
E – ⋯	APR 22	DRINKS		462	4.20		60.95
F – TEA	APR 22	REST'R	G	462	12.00		72.85
G – ⋯	APR 22	PHONE	K	462	0.45		73.30
H – TRANSFER	APR 22	SVCE	L	462	3.40		76.70
J – ⋯	APR 22	APART		462	28.00		104.70
K – LOCAL PHONE CALL	APR 23	⋯	M	462	0.30		105.00
L – ⋯	APR 23	REST'R	D	462	4.50		109.00
M – ⋯	APR 23	CASH		462		109.00	0.00

12 With a partner act out as much of the dialogue in Exercise 11 as you can remember, pointing to items in the bill as you talk about them.

13 Use the bill in Exercise 9 or the bill in Exercise 11. Point to items in the bill, and ask and answer questions like this.

Student A
(guest)
What's this for?
What's this charge?
What does this mean?

What does this letter stand for?

Student B
(hotel cashier)
It's a telephone call from your room.
It's a laundry charge.
It means 'news-stand'. You bought a newspaper from the bookstall that day.
It stands for 'lunch'. You had lunch in the hotel that day.
Etc.

Follow-up

14 Mr A. Fellows stays for the two nights of 21 and 22 July in the Rumboldi Hotel. The room rate is 26000L. per night. He has two breakfasts, each of which costs 4000L. On the evening of 22 July he has dinner at the hotel for 15000L. Also on 22 July he has drinks charged at 2300L, makes a long distance telephone call charged at 2800L. and buys cigarettes charged at 650L. The hotel obtains a theatre ticket for him at 8500L. On the morning of 23 July he buys a newspaper for 200L. The hotel adds a service charge of 10% to the total of all charges.

Write out a bill for Mr Fellows, dated 23 July.

15 Work with a partner. Take part in various transactions that can occur in a hotel, like this:

Student A
Take the part of a *guest* who is staying for two nights in the hotel. Talk to your partner, who represents *various* hotel employees in *various* departments, and obtain the following services:

(a) Reserve a room for two nights.
(b) Have some meals and drinks in the hotel.
(c) Ask for the use of various facilities in the hotel — laundry, photocopying, telephone, hairdressing, etc.
(d) Hand your key in and check out. Check your bill and ask questions as you wish. Pay your bill and say goodbye politely.

Student B
Take the part of *various* hotel employes in *various* departments, as follows:

(a) Reception Clerk. Take A's reservation and tell him the room rate.
(b) Various other employees. Decide how much to charge for each service. Take a note of every service A requests and add it to the 'bill'. You do not need to tell A the price of each service unless he asks about it.
(c) The Reception Clerk at check-out time. Make up A's bill, adding a service charge if you wish. Give A the bill and be ready to explain any points that surprise him. Express goodwill and say goodbye, etc.

16 Work with a partner. For Student A, see below. For Student B see page 186.

Student A

You are the Assistant Manager of the Phoenix Hotel. A guest has come to you with some complaints about his bill.

Listen to the guest (Student B). Try to calm the guest down. Take any action you feel is necessary.

Language reference

Phrases used by guest on checking out:
I'd like to check out, please;   Can I check out, please?
Can I pay by cheque/credit card?;   Do you take Access/Visa/etc.?;   I'll pay cash/pay by cheque/pay by credit card

Questions on reading the bill:
What's this for?;   What's this charge?;   What does this mean?;   What does this letter stand for?

Phrases used by clerk:
I'll get you your bill
How would you like to pay?;   How are you paying?;   Are you paying by (credit card)?
If I could have your card a moment;   Could I see your card a moment, please?;   Do you have your card?
I'm sorry./I'm afraid this credit card has expired/is out of date

Accepting a card or a cheque
That's fine;   That'll do nicely
I'll get you (a receipt, etc.)

Explaining the bill
It's for (a telephone call, etc.);   It's a (laundry charge, etc.);   It means (news-stand, etc.);   It stands for (lunch, etc.)

Simple future with *I'll* for undertakings: I'll get you your bill, etc.
Simple past for explaining bills: You bought a newspaper, etc.

Methods of payment: cheque; credit card; cash; traveller's cheque; foreign currency

Credit cards: Access; Visa
Charge cards: American Express; Diners Club

Note: Although the expression 'credit card' is often used for all cards used to pay a bill, there is in fact a difference between a 'credit card' and a 'charge card' as follows:

A *credit card* is issued free to customers. The customer can choose to pay only part of the total bill which appears on his monthly statement, but must pay interest on the amount of credit given.

A *charge card* requires payment of an annual subscription from customers. The customer must settle the total bill in full each month. A charge card usually has a higher credit limit than a credit card.

Miscellaneous vocabulary

adjustment	mechanized
allowance	minerals
brought forward	notify
carried forward	receipt
cashier	run (through a computer)
charge	service charge
code letter	slip
credit card	sundry
disbursement	tip
drug store	traveller's cheque
expire	unscramble
expiry	update
foreign currency	valid
guarantee	value added tax (VAT)
light refreshment	

Dealing with complaints

To start you off

1 Read the beginnings of some complaints below. As quickly as possible, answer these questions:

Which complaint is
(a) about the condition of the room?
(b) about food?
(c) about something returned to the guest later than promised?
(d) about a disturbance in a neighbouring room?
(e) made by the management, to a guest?

1. Look, I was told I would get my suit back from the dry cleaning by five o'clock and it's now half past six. I absolutely must have it this evening!
2. Can you do something about the people in the next room? They seem to be having a party through there. The noise is driving me crazy.
3. I asked for my steak rare — this steak is so well done it's almost uneatable.
4. As far as I can see it hasn't been cleaned since the last guest left. The bed hasn't been made, the sheets haven't been changed, and the bathroom is in a disgusting mess.
5. I'm sorry, but could we ask you to keep the noise down a little? We've had complaints from some of the other guests who are finding it difficult to sleep.

2 How would you deal (or continue dealing) with the complaints above:

(a) if you were a member of the hotel staff?
(b) if you were the guest?

3 Complete the sentences below. You will hear them spoken by a manager in Exercise 4 after a guest says:

I've telephoned Room Service three times, but my breakfast still hasn't come.

(a) I'm _____ sorry about this, madam. I really must _____.

(b) You should _____ received the breakfast no _____ than five or ten minutes after you _____ it.

(c) The problem may be that they've been rather _____-staffed in the kitchens recently.

(d) But I'll _____ into this, and I'll make _____ that the breakfast is sent to you immediately. Full English breakfast, was it?

(e) _____ well, madam. I'll _____ with this myself, and I'll _____ it sent up to your room _____ away.

Developing the topic

4 Listen to the dialogue. Check your answers to Exercise 3. Then listen again and answer these questions:

(a) What is the guest's complaint?
(b) While listening to the complaint, does the Manager speak at all? What does he say?
(c) What is the first thing he says *after* hearing the complaint?
(d) How does he check that he has understood the complaint?
(e) He apologizes several times during the conversation. What does he say?
(f) What explanation does he give?
(g) What action does he promise?

5 In the dialogue above, the Hotel Manager said:
I'm sorry madam
I'm very sorry about this
I really must apologize

Study the ways of apologizing in the Language Reference section. The Hotel Manager also promised action on the complaint. He said:

I'll have it sent up to your room right away.

Study the ways of 'promising action' in the Language Reference section.

Form replies to the complaints below. Use any suitable phrase of apology, and any suitable phrase promising action. Use the verb in brackets at the end of the sentence. The first one is done as an example.

(a) We've been waiting half an hour for our suitcases. (send up)
  I'm sorry about that, sir. I'll have them sent up right away.
(b) This tablecloth is filthy! Can't you give us another one? (replace)
(c) Why is it taking so long to make our bill up? (make up)

(d) I paid the parking attendant to wash my car, but nobody has washed it. (wash)
(e) I'm sure the sheets on the bed haven't been changed after the last guest. (change)
(f) There's a mistake in the bill. We didn't have dinner here last night. (check)
(g) We arranged for an extra bed to be put in the room for our young son. But there's only one double bed here. (attend to)

With a partner, practise making and responding to the complaints above, with suitable apologies and promises of action.

6 Look at some of the main 'rules' for handling complaints.

(a) Listen carefully to the complaint.
(b) Do not interrupt.
(c) Wait until the person has completely finished.
(d) Apologize.
(e) Speak normally.
(f) Summarize the complaint.
(g) Explain what action will be taken, and how quickly.
(h) If the guest is angry, aim to remove the scene to somewhere private.

Which of these rules are most important? In groups, decide on the three most important rules.

Which rule do you think is most difficult to follow?

Now match the additional sentences below with rules (a)–(h) above. They are not in the same order as the rules.

1. If you repeat the main points of a complaint, you make sure that there is no misunderstanding about the reason for the complaint; and saying the main points calmly helps to cool down the situation.
2. Before saying anything at all, be certain that the guest has completely finished talking and is not just pausing for breath.
3. A short clear apology should be the first thing you offer the guest. This must come before any explanations or reasons.
4. Do not let your voice rise to match the voice of the guest. This will only lead to more argument.
5. Make clear what *you* will do. Give the guest a definite time so that he understands that his complaint will be attended to.
6. An interruption will cause the guest to carry on louder and longer.
7. It is important to show that you are giving the guest full attention.
8. This could be an office, or an empty lounge. Try to find a place where there is no barrier (table or desk) between you and the guest.

121

7 Read the dialogue below between a Duty Manager (DM) and a guest.

GUEST: Are you the Manager?

DM: I'm the Duty Manager. And you're Mr Cane from the Seaways Group, aren't you? Can I help you?

GUEST: You'd better. My suitcases have been stolen and I want them back, quick!

DM: Let's go into my office, and you can tell me exactly what's happened. (*they go into the office*)

GUEST: Two suitcases. They've been stolen from outside my room ...

DM: Yes.

GUEST: I put them out this morning for the Porter to collect. He was supposed to take them down to the Seaways Tour bus. But I've just been down to the bus, and there's a pile of suitcases there, but mine aren't among them. They must have been stolen.

DM: I see. What time did you put them out?

GUEST: About seven-thirty.

DM: And can you tell me what they look like?

GUEST: They're large, soft grey leather suitcases with Seaways stickers on them. Look, I want some action on this!

DM: Yes, of course Mr Cane. I'm very sorry about this. Just let me get clear what happened. You left two suitcases outside your door at half-past seven, for the Porter to take down to the tour bus. You've been to the bus, and there's no sign of the suitcases.

GUEST: Right.

DM: Right then Mr Cane. It's possible that the suitcases have been put down in the wrong place. So the first thing I'm going to do is contact the Porter, the Head Porter and the Tour Courier. Together we'll check the hotel and the bus thoroughly. I'll also contact the Hotel Security Officer, and we'll see then if we have to contact the police.

In the dialogue above, how does the Duty Manager do the following things? Give words and sentences as necessary:

(a) move the scene of the complaint to a less public place
(b) show that he is listening carefully
(c) apologize
(d) summarize the complaint
(e) give a possible explanation of the event
(f) tell the guest what action will be taken

Now act out the dialogue with a partner, without looking at the text of the dialogue. You can put the ideas in your own words, and include ideas of your own, but try to include stages (a)–(f), above.

8 Create and act out with a partner a dialogue based on the following situation.

A guest comes up to Mrs Dale, the Duty Manager, complaining angrily about the Hall Porter's Department. Since there are other guests present, the Duty Manager invites the guest to come to her office to talk things over.

The guest tells the Duty Manager that the Hall Porter yesterday promised to obtain theatre tickets for a show in the city. He says that today, when he went to collect the tickets there was another porter on duty. The porter could not find any tickets for the guest, and could not find any record of the request for tickets. It seems that the porter on duty today did not believe that the guest had made any request for tickets. The guest says that the tickets were promised, that he has made arrangements to go to the theatre that night, and that it is the hotel's job to provide the tickets.

The Duty Manager apologizes, summarizes the complaint, and says that the Hall Porter is off duty today. However, she knows where he is. She promises to telephone him immediately and find out about the tickets. She says that if the hotel has made a mistake, she will personally contact the theatre and do her best to reserve tickets for this evening's performance.

☐☐

9 Listen to the three dialogues on the tape. In two of the dialogues, the hotel employee deals with the complaint quite well, but in one of the dialogues he/she deals with it badly. Fill in the tables below. (Note: not all the boxes can be filled for each dialogue.)

	DIALOGUE 1	DIALOGUE 2	DIALOGUE 3
Scene of complaint is moved to:			
The problem			
Words or phrases of apology (several in each dialogue):			
Reason or explanation:			
Action to be taken now:			

123

In which dialogue does the employee deal badly with the complaint? What should the employee have done?

Write out the dialogue to show how the complaint should have been dealt with.

10 Use the 'rules' for dealing with complaints, and any suitable language from previous exercises, or from the Language Reference section. Act out with a partner complaints, apologies, explanations and details of action to be taken, for any of the following situations.

A guest finds that some items of clothing are missing from returned laundry.

A guest has been disturbed by a chambermaid coming to clean the room.

A guest has not been attended to quickly by staff at the reception desk.

Water leaking through a ceiling has damaged a guest's property.

11 Sometimes the *hotel management* has to complain to *guests* about their behaviour.

Listen to the three examples of this on the tape, then answer the questions below.

(a) What have the guests done in Dialogue 1? Dialogue 2? Dialogue 3?
(b) What sentences in the dialogues are polite ways of saying:
  — *You must change the way you ... (do something).*
  — *You aren't allowed to ... (do something).*
  — *We want payment for some of the damage you have done.*
  — *We'll keep your luggage if you don't pay.*
  — *Stop making so much noise.*
(c) In two of the dialogues, the Manager suggests a hotel service which guests could use. What services does he suggest, and why does he make the suggestion?

12 In the Language Reference section, study the types of polite sentences that can be used by a hotel manager when making complaints to guests. These sentences are usually *firm requests* to guests to change their behaviour.

The 'message' behind the polite language must be clear. In the following polite sentences, what is the real 'message' that the Manager is trying to give to a guest?

(a) I'm sorry sir, but you actually aren't allowed into the dinner-dance unless you're wearing a tie ...
(b) I'm afraid the barman is unable to serve you any further drinks this evening, sir.
(c) We'll have to ask you to leave this lounge, sir, I'm afraid. We have to consider the other guests, you see ...
(d) Unfortunately we can't extend your stay any longer. I'm sure you'll understand the reasons ...

Now *you* try to make polite sentences from the following 'messages':

(e) We won't let you stay in this hotel again!
(f) Stop smoking!
(g) Be quiet!
(h) We will take you to court if you don't pay!
(i) You're annoying the other guests! Stop it!

With a partner, act out a conversation which includes any of the situations above, and any of the *polite* phrases you have seen in this exercise.

Follow-up

13 Choose any situation from earlier in the unit in which a guest complains to a manager, or else take a new subject for complaint. For example:

— a suit or dress you sent for dry cleaning has been ruined

— a chambermaid has told you that if you want the room to be cleaned twice a day you will have to clean it yourself
— you have complained about the heating in your room every day since you arrived, and nothing has been done

With other students, form a group, A, B, C and D.

Students A and B prepare and act out a dialogue in which the Manager deals with the situation in the wrong way, and simply makes the guest more and more angry.

Students C and D prepare and act out the dialogue, but with the Manager dealing with the situation in a better way.

For both dialogues, invite comments from other students in your class about how well the Manager has handled the situation.

14 Proceed as for Exercise 13, but this time, choose a situation in which a manager has to complain to a guest, or to prevent a guest from doing something. You can use ideas from Exercise 12, or a new idea. For example:

— a businessman from the Far East wants the bill sent to his firm in Indonesia for settlement.
— a guest insists on taking some friends, who are not registered at the hotel, into his room late at night. It seems likely that their aim is to get free accommodation
— a guest is observed removing valuable hotel property from the hotel

15 Work with a partner.

Student A
Write a letter to a hotel manager complaining about the service provided by the hotel during your recent stay. You are angry because: the service was slow; the room was not properly cleaned either before or during your stay; the receptionist seemed unwilling to answer your enquiries, and no porters were available to help with your luggage. You say that although you have stayed at the hotel several times in the past, you are unwilling to come again unless there is some guarantee of improvement.

Student B
As Hotel Manager, write back to the guest. Apologize for the problems that the guest had during her stay. Explain that unfortunately you had to take on temporary staff during the period of the guests' stay owing to the illness of some long-serving staff. Say that the situation is now back to normal, and that you are now fully confident that you can provide your normal standard of service. Apologize once again. Say that you hope that the guest will return for a further stay, and that she will let the management know immediately if the service is unsatisfactory in any way.

126

16 Work with a partner. Student A looks at the information below. Student B looks at the information on page 186.

Student A

You come as a guest to the hotel. You arrive tired because of a delay in your flight. You discover that the room you reserved has been let to another guest, and the room you are given is very noisy. You sleep badly, and you are wakened early in the morning by an unwanted wake-up call. At 09.30, when you are at last sleeping peacefully, the chambermaid comes into the room to clean it, waking you up again. You complain to the manager (Student B) about all these problems, and demand better service.

Language reference

Expressions used by guests in complaining
I was told ... (but) ...;   We arranged ... (but) ...;   I asked for ... (but) ...;
I've telephoned three times ... (but) ... ...;   I paid for ... (but) ...
Can you do something about ...?/Can't you do something about ...?
This (item) is dirty/in a mess/disgraceful/disgusting!, etc.
What's the meaning of this?
What nonsense is this?
I've never (heard such rudeness/seen such a mess, etc.)!
I asked for X, not Y!

Expressions used by hotel staff in dealing with complaints

Apologizing
I'm sorry
I'm very/extremely sorry (about this/that)
I really must apologize
I do apologize
(Notes: *We* may be used by the Manager instead of *I*. *Sir* or *madam* may be added)

Moving the scene to somewhere private
Let's go into my office;   Why don't we go through to the lounge?;   Would you like to come through to the office?;   (very firm) ... in my office, if you don't mind

Promising or explaining action to be taken
(getting someone else to do something)
I'll *have* (it *sent up* right away, etc.)
I'll *get* (it *attended* to immediately etc.)

I'll *make sure* (it's *brought* to you immediately, etc.)
(taking personal action)
I'll deal with this myself; I'll look into this . . .; I'll sort out (this mistake, etc.); What I'm going to do now is . . .; The first thing I'm going to do is . . .

Showing attention to what the guest is saying
Yes; I see; (plus nods of the head, eye contact, etc.)

Giving a reason or explanation
There seems to have been; There's obviously been a misunderstanding; We've been rather short-staffed recently; It's possible that . . . (X has happened)

Promising an improvement in service, promising to try harder (written responses)
I can assure you that we'll (do our best to) return to our normal standards of service; We are confident that we shall be able to provide our normal standard of service, etc.

Examples of firm requests from manager to guests

The Manager may refer to rules or accepted procedures
I'm afraid guests aren't allowed to . . .
Our regulations don't permit . . .
The hotel has the right to . . ., etc.

The Manager may 'ask for permission' to make the request; normally he will use 'we'
Can we ask you to (settle this bill now, etc.)?

The Manager may say that things are 'necessary' or 'impossible'
I'm afraid *we must ask you* to (leave the hotel, etc.)
We *will have to* (call the police unless . . ., etc.)
The hotel *cannot/is unable to* (extend your stay, etc.)

Words expressing damage
ruined; smash; beyond repair; broken; damaged

Words expressing unclean conditions or bad service
disgusting; mess; filthy; disgraceful

Words expressing anger at a foolish situation
ridiculous; absurd

Miscellaneous vocabulary

admit (a person to a place)
apology
barrier
compliments of the house
cool down (a situation)
cornflakes
court (of law)
cowshed
dinner-dance
disturbance
drive someone crazy
extend
guide-dog

inconvenience (v)
interrupt
keep noise down
leak
long-serving
look into something
rare (of steak)
regulation
scene
short-staffed
summarize
talk things over
thorough
well-done (of steak)

Conference facilities

To start you off

1 This unit is concerned with facilities for conferences and other types of formal meeting. You can see words for different types of meeting below, but the definitions for them are in the wrong order.
Match the words on the left with the definitions on the right.

(a) CONFERENCE   1. A formal presentation by an expert. It is sometimes followed by questions from the audience.

(b) LECTURE   2. The general word for a formal meeting or series of meetings between people who share the same interests. It often involves both general lectures and discussion in smaller groups.

(c) CONGRESS   3. Sometimes organized as part of a conference, this is a meeting of a smaller group in which people work on practical problems and help each other to gain new knowledge. Often there are no more than 30−40 participants.

(d) CONVENTION   4. A large meeting or series of meetings of experts in a particular field — often experts from different countries. More formal than a conference.

(e) WORKSHOP   5. A large conference of people who do a particular job or who belong to a particular political party. The word is used especially in America.

(f) SEMINAR   6. A meeting of a small group (usually under 30 people) to learn from a expert; less concerned with practical or group tasks than a workshop.

2 Below you can see a list of items which may be needed in a conference. Match them with the pictures 1−13 which follow.

(a) overhead projector   (d) photocopier
(b) tape recorder   (e) slide projector
(c) video recorder   (f) whiteboard

(g) film projector
(h) projection screen
(i) word processor
(j) closed circuit TV

(k) flip-chart
(l) lectern
(m) gavel

1

2

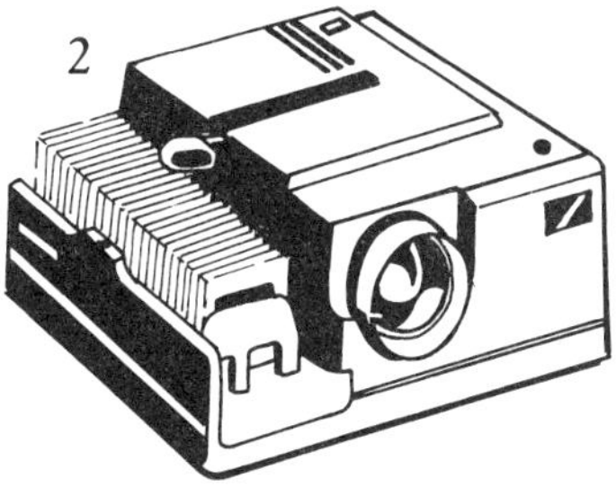

3

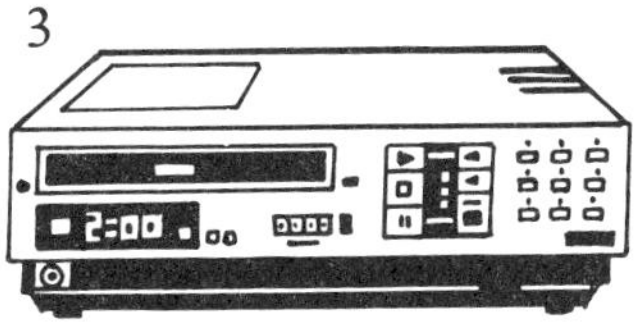

4

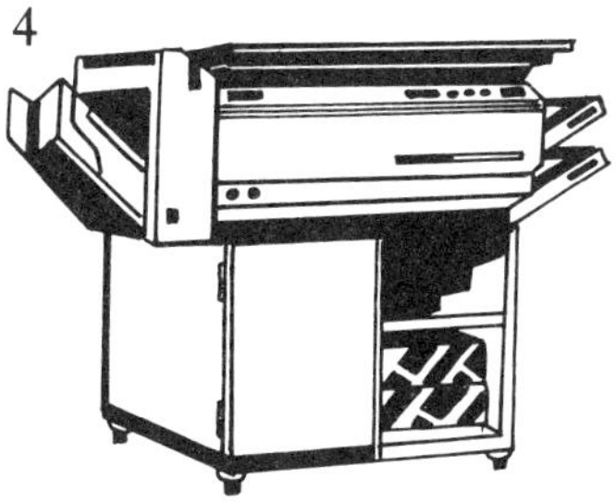

5

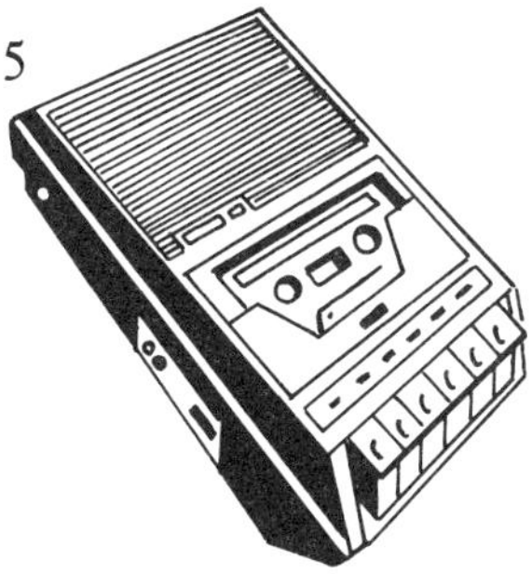

6

7

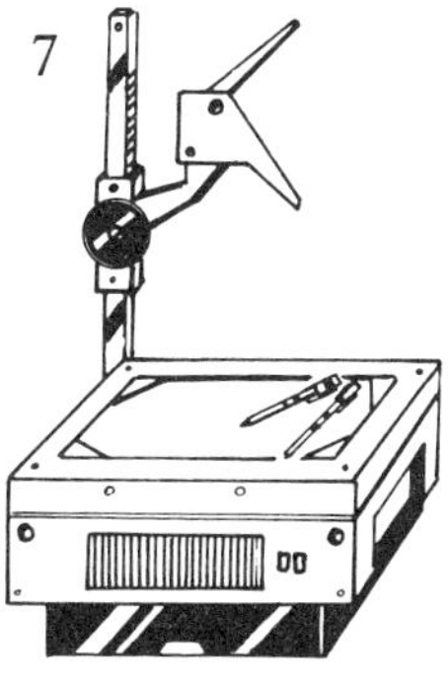

8

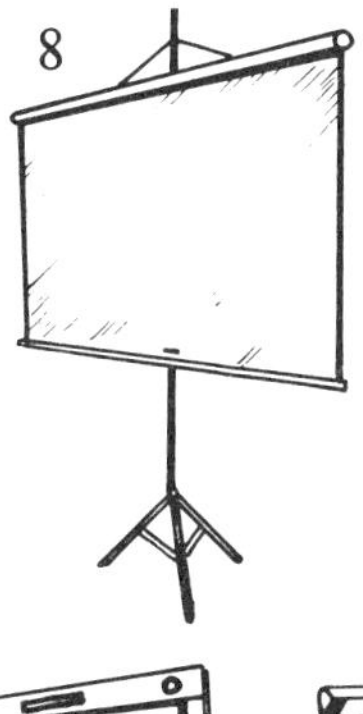

9

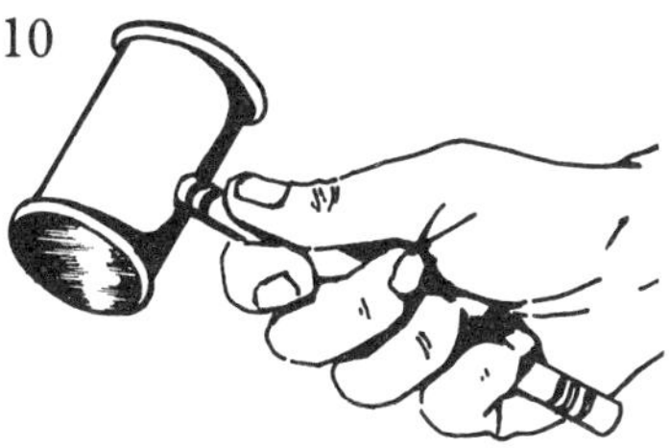

11

A1

12

10

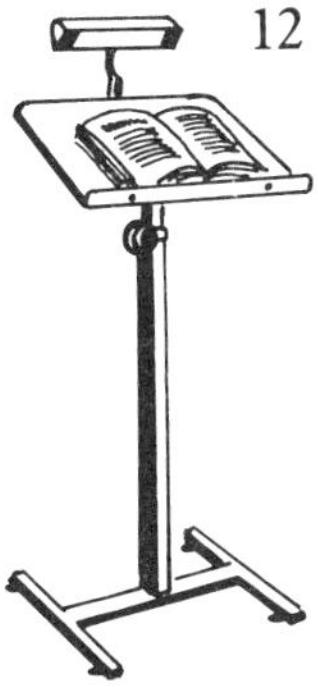

13

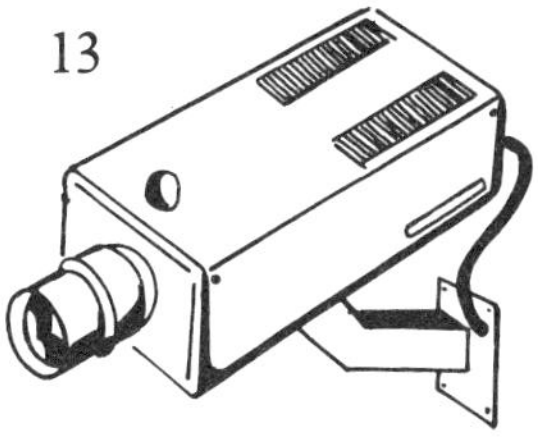

3 Match the definitions below with the pieces of equipment in the previous exercise. (For example, (a) is a definition of a lectern.

(a) a sloping table used for holding a book, or lecture notes, when speaking to an audience or reading aloud
(b) a machine which makes photographic copies of any drawn or printed page
(c) a machine which records sounds, speech or music, and allows these sounds to be played back to a listener
(d) a machine like a typewriter which lets you see what you write on a kind of TV screen
(e) a machine for passing light through a piece of film in order to show a still (unmoving) picture on a screen
(f) machine for passing light through moving film in order to show moving pictures on a screen
(g) a machine which records moving scenes or pictures and allows them to be played back on a TV screen
(h) a television system which sends pictures by wire to a particular audience in a particular place
(i) a piece of white cloth, plastic, etc. on which pictures can be shown
(j) a machine which shows on a screen words or diagrams written on a piece of clear film
(k) a kind of book with large pages (suitable for drawing diagrams, etc.) which can be turned over when a new, blank page is required
(l) a smooth white surface on which words can be written with a special pen
(m) a small hammer which a person in charge of a meeting uses, knocking it against the table in order to get attention

4 What are these?

(a) A/V equipment
(b) OHP
(c) VCR
(d) PA system

5 Fill in the sentences below. You will hear them in a dialogue between a conference organiser and a hotel manager. Use words from this list:

seats   seating (×2)   sound   partitions   built-in   single
equipment   circuit   acoustics   exhibition   centre

(a) Basically, we have a multi-purpose conference _____ with _____ for over 450 delegates.
(b) Our main auditorium _____ 350 people.

132

(c) The smaller conference rooms have a _____ capacity of about 55 each.
(d) We have _____-proof folding _____ between the conference rooms. These can be opened up to form a _____ large room.
(e) The auditorium has _____ audiovisual _____.
(f) We can provide a closed _____ television link-up from the auditorium to the smaller conference halls.
(g) You'll find that both the auditorium and the conference rooms have excellent _____.
(h) There's also an _____ hall, for display purposes.

Developing the topic

6 Dr Milne is a conference organiser for the Association of Psychological Researchers (APR). Listen to his conversation with the Manager of the Nova Hotel. Check your answers to Exercise 5. Then answer the questions below.

(a) How many participants is Dr Milne expecting at the conference?
(b) What event will be held in the hotel before the APR conference?
(c) What event will be held after the APR conference?
(d) What does the Manager say about (i) the seating capacity of the auditorium, and (ii) the area of the two smaller conference rooms?
(e) What translation facilities will Dr Milne require, and for what languages?
(f) What does the Manager give Dr Milne to take away and study?
(g) What does the Manager offer to do at the end of the conversation?

7 Look at the notes Dr Milne makes after his conversation with the Hotel Manager.

```
Nova Hotel
1 large auditorium (seating capacity 350)
2 Conference rooms (each 35 square metres)-
Can be joined to form one large room, total
Seating capacity about 110
1 exhibition room (30 square metres).
```

What does he write in his report when he gets back to his office? Complete the sentences below.

133

The Nova Hotel .... auditorium with .... of 350. In addition, there are two .... Each of them has .... of 35 square metres. They can be joined to form one large room with .... of about 110. There is also an exhibition room with .... of 30 square metres.

Now look at the notes which Dr Milne makes about the facilities in another hotel.

Galaxy Hotel
1 fairly large auditorium (seating capacity 250)
1 large general-purpose room (about 110 square metres - could be used as an additional lecture room, seating capacity about 120.
2 smaller rooms for exhibitions or small groups (20 square metres each, would seat about 15 each).

Write a report about the Galaxy Hotel, similar to the one Dr Milne wrote about the Nova Hotel above.

Which hotel do you think Dr Milne will choose?

8 Look again at the notes for the Nova Hotel and the Galaxy Hotel. *Compare* the hotels, answering these questions in complete sentences.

(a) Which auditorium is bigger — the Nova auditorium or the Galaxy auditorium?
(b) Which hotel has a greater total seating capacity?
(c) Which hotel offers the larger floor area for conference activities (not counting the auditoriums)?
(d) Which hotel offers more rooms suitable for exhibitions?
(e) You are organizing a conference. You are looking for a hotel which will fit in with the following plans:
   — You must be able to hold two lectures and two small seminars all at the same time
   — Your only exhibition will be a small exhibition of books, at the back of the main auditorium
   Which hotel is more suitable for your plans?
   (Begin: *The _____ Hotel is more suitable because we can have one lecture in* ...., *another in* ...., *etc.*)

9   Now look at the details for two other hotels — the Mercury Hotel and the Jupiter Hotel.

Mercury Hotel
1 auditorium (seats 180)
1 general-purpose room (seats 100, 70 square metres), can be partitioned into 2 rooms (each seating 40)
2 seminar rooms (each seats 30, each 30 square metres)
1 exhibition room (50 square metres, no seats)

Jupiter Hotel
1 auditorium (seats 110)
1 auditorium (seats 100)
2 conference rooms (each seats 70, each 60 square metres)
2 seminar/exhibition rooms (each seats 40, each 35 square metres)

You are a conference organizer. The conference will include only two general lectures (one at the beginning and one at the end of the conference). The most important activities will be practical workshops and seminars in small groups, but there will also be a large permanent exhibition. There will be 120 participants.

Write a short report comparing the two hotels. Compare them in terms of:

(a) seating capacity
(b) size of the main auditorium
(c) total number of rooms for non-lecturing activities
(d) floor area (not counting the auditoriums)

Include a conclusion, saying which hotel is better for your purposes, and why.

[QO]

10   Dr Milne has arranged for the APR conference to be held at the Nova Hotel. He is talking to the Hotel Manager to make sure that everything is ready.

Listen to the conversation. Look at the checklist below.

— Put a double tick (√√) for items that are ready, checked and in place for the conference.
— Put a single tick (√) for items in the conversation that are still to come, or still to be tested.
— Cross out items which will not be needed.
— Leave blank any items which the conversation does not cover. Have the speakers forgotten about anything?

whiteboard ☐   whiteboard pens ☐   pointer ☐   cloth ☐

flip chart ☐   felt-tip pens ☐

overhead projector □   transparencies □   spare bulb □

slide projector □   extra cartridge □

projection screen □

film projector □   empty reel □

tape recorder □   spare spool □   microphone □   tape □

PA-system □   amplifier □   microphone □   loudspeakers □

simultaneous □   earphones □
translation
equipment

lighting □   dimmer □   lectern light □   spotlight □

air conditioning/
heating/ventilation □

closed circuit TV □   VCR □   camera □

photocopying □

typewriter □   typing paper □   carbon paper □ correcting fluid □

notice board □   drawing pins □   paper clips □   stapler □

pencils □   gavel □ notepads □ name tags □   folders □

11 Listen to the conversation again, and answer these questions.

(a) Why did the slide projector not work immediately?
(b) Why will interpreting equipment not be necessary?
(c) Where is the empty reel for the film projector?
(d) Why does Dr Milne think the gavel will be needed?

12 Complete the sentences below with words in this list. Some of them are from the check-list in Exercise 9, while others are from earlier in the unit.

VCR   technician   translation   screen   air-conditioning
photocopies   transparencies   microphone   acoustics
PA system   congress   loudspeakers

(a) We'll need some additional _____ for the overhead projector.
(b) We've got a film projector, but unfortunately we haven't got a _____ to show the film on.
(c) The lecture theatre gets very hot if the _____ isn't working.

(d) One of our staff-trainers is giving a demonstration to a group of hotel receptionists this afternoon. We'll need a _____ to record the demonstration.

(e) This equipment is so complicated that I've asked for a _____ to come and operate it.

(f) This room has very good _____ — even without a microphone you can hear every word perfectly.

(g) One of our speakers gave his lecture in Chinese. Fortunately, a simultaneous _____ was available.

(h) Could you please make twenty _____ of this page? I'd like everyone at the meeting to have the information in front of them.

(i) 'Can you test the _____ before the lecture starts?' 'OK, I'll do it now. *Testing, one, two, three, four ...*'

(j) Our conference room is well-equipped, with a good _____. So it will be easy to make announcements to all the participants.

(k) The reason the system works so well is that we have high-quality _____ placed at the front, middle and back of the room.

(l) Next week there will be a _____ of brain surgeons, with participants from many different countries.

Follow-up

13 Describe to other students the conference facilities in any hotel you know.

14 With a group of other students, plan a conference for students and teachers of *English for Hotel Workers.*

Discuss the number of participants there are likely to be, and the kind of activities which participants will find useful. Make a list of the facilities you need (rooms and equipment).

Report on what your group has decided to the rest of your class. Find out if other students agree with your group's ideas.

15 For Student A's part see below. For Student B's part see page 186.

Student A
You are the manager of the Great Ship Hotel. Student B wants to find out about your conference facilities, and to negotiate suitable rates with you.

Here are some parts of your conference brochure.

> # Are You Planning an Important Conference or Congress?
>
> *Come to us at the Great Ship Hotel!*
>
> Our atmosphere is unique, with decor and fittings of the great ships of the past. But our conference facilities are the most modern and versatile you will find anywhere.
>
> Many well-known companies have already made their advance bookings. Why not get in touch with us and find out more?

Plan of facilities

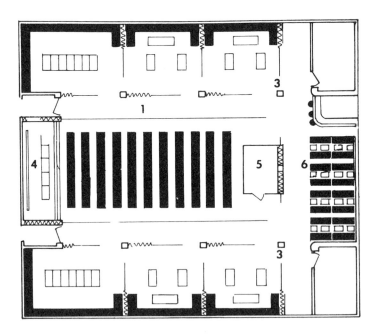

1. Multi-purpose conference hall. Can be extended to include side rooms, using soundproof folding partitions. Space at the sides has large glass screens for exhibitions.
2. Main auditorium. This is the centre of the multi-purpose hall, and seats 124. If desired this can be used as a cinema.
3. Auxiliary rooms. On either side of the main conference hall there is space for 110. This space can be added to the main auditorium, or divided by folding partitions into six smaller rooms, the smallest of which seats 26.
4. Chairman's platform. On the chairman's platform there is a table for five speakers. Behind it there is a projection screen.
5. Film projection room. This has one 35mm and one 16mm projector, as well as a slide projector.
6. The bar/coffee room. This has a seating capacity of 40.

Conference equipment
Every seat in the auditorium has a writing table and a microphone for use during debates.

The rooms at the sides have their own conference equipment which can be used either together with that of the main auditorium or separately.

The centre has a video recorder, camera and seven monitor TV sets for recording presentations and viewing them again. Speakers' own videos can also be shown.

The projection room has both film and slide projectors.

Both 8 and 16mm colour films and slides can be viewed through the TV monitor sets. All normal conference equipment is available, including overhead projectors for transparencies, a photocopier, flip charts, word processing, etc.

Movable equipment
2 8mm film projectors   3 projection screens
8 overhead projectors   4 tape recorders
2 VCRs   9 flip charts

Fixed equipment
1 35mm film projector
1 16mm film projector
equipment for simultaneous interpreting

Rates
Negotiable, depending on the number of participants staying in the hotel. For non-residents, basic hire from $1000 per day. Closed circuit TV, interpreting equipment, copying service, extra A/V equipment, and secretarial services charged separately.

Language reference

Types of meeting
conference; lecture; congress; convention; workshop; seminar

Equipment needed at conferences
electrical equipment:
overhead projector; tape recorder; video recorder; photocopier; slide projector; film projector; word processor; closed circuit TV; amplifier; dimmer; VCR; spare bulb; microphone; lectern light; loudspeaker; spotlight; camera; audiovisual equipment (or A/V equipment); OHP; PA system; air conditioning; heating; ventilation; simultaneous translation equipment; earphones
presentation equipment:
whiteboard; flip chart; lectern; transparencies; slide cartridge; spare spool; gavel; pointer; empty reel; projection screen
stationery and writing equipment:
felt-tip pens; marker pens; chalk; typing paper; drawing pins; carbon paper; paper clips; notepads; duster; eraser; stapler; folders; name tags; bluetack; sellotape; cloth (to erase whiteboard writing); correcting fluid (to erase typing errors)

Vocabulary related to conference rooms
multi-purpose; conference centre; auditorium; capacity; sound-proof; folding partition; exhibition hall; seating; seating capacity; acoustics; air-conditioning; heating; ventilation; seat (v)

Other vocabulary related to conferences
simultaneous translation; translator; interpreter; debate; delegate; participant

Structures of measurement
have a seating capacity of ...; have an area of ... square metres

Structures of comparison
be bigger/more suitable, etc. than ...
have a greater seating capacity than ...
have a larger floor area than ...

Miscellaneous vocabulary

capacity	negotiable	versatile
expert	practical	view (v)
formal	presentation	whine
if desired	series	
involve	sloping	

UNIT 17

Careers

To start you off

1 Below you can see some of the people who work in the Ibex Hotel chain, and the jobs they do. How would people come to have these jobs in your country? What kind of experience and qualifications would they have?

1

2

3

4

5

6

2 Complete the sentences below. You will hear them in an interview with one of the people above, on the tape.

(a) I became _____ in hotel work because my mother is in the hotel _____.

(b) I _____ French and German.

(c) After I _____ school, I went to a Hotel College, and did a Hotel Reception _____.

(d) My first _____ was _____ trainee Receptionist in the Ibex Hotel in Brighton.

(e) Before I got my _____ job as Senior Receptionist, I _____ two years at the Paris Grand Ibex Hotel.

Developing the topic

3 Check your answers to Exercise 2. Then listen to interviews with three of the people above. Write notes about them in the table below. Put in dates and times when they are given.

	Una	Ahmed	Pedro
Why did they choose to do hotel work?			
What courses have they taken in hotel work (if any)?			
What certificates or diplomas have they got (if any)?			
What hotel jobs have they done?			
How long have they been with Ibex?			
What foreign languages do they speak?			
What is their ambition?			

4 A Personnel Officer for the Phoenix Hotel chain has met the three people above at a Hotel and Tourism Conference. He wants to recruit good staff for the Phoenix chain, and he is trying to find out about their careers. Here are some of the questions he asks Una.

How long have you been with Ibex?
Have you taken any courses in hotel work?
Have you got any diplomas or certificates?
What positions have you held so far?
Have you worked in any large hotels?
Have you made any plans for the future?

With a partner, ask and answer the questions for Una, Ahmed and Pedro, using the information in the interviews, and in the notes above.

5 When applying for a job, people often have to send a summary of their career — their education, the jobs they have done, etc. In Britain, this is called a *Curriculum Vitae* (or CV for short). In America it is called a *resumé*.
Here is an example of a CV for Kevin Bell. Answer the questions under the CV as quickly as possible.

Name	Kevin John Bell
Date and place of birth	2 February 1968, Leytonstone, London
Marital status	Single
Nationality	British
Education	Leyton Park Primary (1973-1979) Leyton Senior High School (1979-1984) Leytonstone Technical College, course in Food Service (1986-present)
Qualifications	Certificate of Secondary Education (Mathematics, English, French) I expect to obtain the Certificate in Food Service this year.
Practical experience	Bus boy, Park Hotel, Bristol, 1984-1985 Trainee waiter, Ibex Hotel, Gatwick (1985-present)
Languages	French

(a) Where was Kevin born?
(b) Is Kevin married?
(c) Did Kevin take a course in hotel work while he was at High School?
(d) Has Kevin passed all his exams in the course he is doing now?

(e) What qualifications is Kevin hoping to get?
(f) What was his first hotel job?
(g) What foreign language can he speak?

6 In the interviews, we heard Ahmed talking about his career in hotels, up to the point where he is a trainee Assistant Manager with Ibex.
Ahmed's career has now gone a little further. You can see his CV below, but the details, (a)–(h) are in the wrong order.
Match the headings 1–8 on the left with the information (a)–(h) on the right.

1. Name

2. Date and place of birth

3. Marital status

4. Nationality

5. Education

6. Qualifications

7. Practical experience

8. Languages

(a) Dual Egyptian/British

(b) Arabic (mother tongue)
English (fluent, speech and writing)
French (good spoken French)

(c) Hotel Technical School Diploma (1977)

(d) 15 June 1962, Alexandria

(e) Hall Porter, Sea Hotel, Alexandria, (July–December 1977)
Junior Receptionist, Sea Hotel (1978–79)
Receptionist, Pyramid Hotel, Cairo (1979–83)
Trainee Assistant Manager, Ibex Hotel, Cairo (1983–84), then Ibex Hotel, Glasgow (1984–86)
Deputy Assistant Manager, Ibex Hotel, Newcastle (1986–89)

(f) Ahmed Anwar Suleiman Husseini

(g) Married (wife British)

(h) West Alexandria Elementary and Intermediate Schools (1968–74)
Gamel Abdul Nasser Hotel Technical School (1974–77)

7 Ahmed sees these advertisements in the *Catering Times*. Which advertisement do you think will interest him most?

8 Below, you can see Ahmed's letter of application for the job of Assistant Manager at *The Inn on the Lake*. Some words are missing. Can you fill them in from this list?

recommendation	curriculum vitae	reply	post
responsibilities	background	concerned	challenge
qualities	success	advertisement	employer

```
                                        Ibex Hotel
                                        Cumberland Street
                                        Newcastle-upon-Tyne
                                        Northumbria
                                        NE34 2EG


                                        1 February 1990
```

```
Mr R Roger
Manager
The Inn on the Lake
Shorne
Gravesend
Kent
```

Dear Mr Roger

I am writing in ① _____ to your ② _____ concerning the
③ _____ of Assistant Manager. I enclose my ④ _____ _____ ,
together with a ⑤ _____ from my present ⑥ _____ .

As you will see from my CV, I have a thorough ⑦ _____ in all
hotel departments, including managerial ⑧ _____ in my present
post with Ibex hotels. My work has been particularly ⑨ _____
with conference and banqueting operations.

I believe I have the personal ⑩ _____ to contribute to the
11 _____ of The Inn on the Lake, and would look forward to
taking up the exciting ⑫ _____ which the post offers.

Yours sincerely

Ahmed Husseini

Ahmed Husseini

Enclosures: 2

```
┌────┐
│ ⌒⌒ │
└────┘
```

9 Listen to the interview when Ahmed is interviewed for the job at the Inn on the Lake.

(a) Fill in these questions that are asked at the interview.
   1. Why do you want to . . . . ?
   2. What experience have you had of . . . . ?
   3. What would you say are the main things . . . . ?
   4. Is there anything else . . . . ?
   5. What kind of accommodation . . . . ?
(b) What does Ahmed consider to be the most important things in an Assistant Manager's job?
   1. . . . .
   2. . . . .
   3. . . . .
(c) What type of accommodation is offered?
   1. . . . .
   2. . . . .
(d) What kind of accommodation does Ahmed want? . . . .
(e) What is the starting salary? . . . .

Try to act out the interview between Ahmed and the Hotel Manager, using the questions and answers above to guide you.

10 Read the biographical information below about Kristina Spirios. Then write out a CV for her.

Kristina Spirios was born in Nicosia, Cyprus, in 1963, and has dual Cypriot/British nationality. When she was eleven, her family moved to Manchester, where she attended Canal Street Comprehensive School, obtaining her General Certificate of Education, with 'ordinary' grades in English, Mathematics and French. She always spoke Greek at home.

   After leaving school in 1979 she worked for two years on a farm. From 1981–83 she worked as a general assistant in the Lea Park Hotel, Manchester (most departments, including the hotel gardens). Towards the end of 1983 she joined the Ibex Hotel, Liverpool, as trainee housekeeper, becoming a Floor Housekeeper there in 1984. In 1986 she moved to Amsterdam to become Deputy Housekeeper at the Ibex Hotel there. The Ibex chain has agreed to sponsor her for further training in Britain next year, where she will study for her Diploma in Hotel and Catering Administration.

11 Look at advertisements for jobs which might interest Kristina (after she gets her Diploma), Kevin, Una, or Pedro.

DEPUTY HOUSEKEEPER
(MALE/FEMALE)

required to assist the Head Housekeeper and in her absence to take control of this vital department.
A background in luxury operations, together with a sound management approach, is essential. Craft Trainer Award an advantage.

Please apply in writing to:
Miss P McDonald, Head Housekeeper
Cliveden, Taplow, Berks SL6 0JF

HVCT45 730

HEAD RECEPTIONIST

We are looking for an outstanding leader for our reception department in our very busy, newly refurbished 90 bedroomed hotel in Harrow. The successful candidate must be:

★ **Very smart**
★ **Demonstrative**
★ **Communicative**
★ **A Good Trainer with an ability to work very well with everyone.**

The position will lead quickly to a front office Manager's position where a duty management role will become an important feature of your work.
Candidates will have gained wide experience of computerised front office administration, particularly the WELCOME system.
The remuneration package will reflect the importance we attach to this position.

If you think you can match what we are looking for, please contact:

Anne Hill, Personnel Department
Monksdene Hotel, Gayton Road
Harrow, Middlesex HA1 2NT
with a recent photograph and full C.V.
telephone: (01) 427 2899

FVCD45-167 ●

MANAGERS – LONDON – £11K
...ed 20-25, applicants for this appointment should ...ss flair, initiative and excellent skills in customer ...ations.
The unit is based in the city, and headed by a large International Company, but it has exceptional individual qualities.

GENERAL MANAGER – SWITZERLAND – NEG
This International Deluxe Hotel is looking to appoint a standards orientated General Manager who has experience of working with first class continental hotels. Applicants should be of a Swiss Nationality or hold a C visa.

FOOD BEVERAGE MANAGERS CAIRO/MID EAST – NEG
We have a number of exciting opportunities for young Managers looking for a challenging career move. Only those who have experience, motivation and the commitment to achieve, will be considered for these positions.

132 Cromwell Road, London SW7 4HA.   Tel: 01-370 00

TEWKESBURY HALL HOTEL
Is the latest addition to **Select Country Hotels Ltd**

Select Country Hotels Limited

To enable us to provide the standards expected of this luxury hotel we are looking to recruit the following staff:

RESTAURANT MANAGER
HEAD WAITER
WAITING STAFF

The hotel has a 40 cover restaurant offering classical modern English cuisine, and banqueting for up to 180 people. We are offering the ideal candidate an excellent salary, live in accommodation if required and the opportunity of growing with the leading country house hotel group.

Apply in writing to:

David Chapman, General Manager
Tewkesbury Hall Hotel
Puckrup, Tewkesbury GL20 6EL
Tel: 0684 296200

RVCQ45 666

Write out a letter of application from Kristina, Kevin, Una or Pedro for one of the jobs above. Then with a partner, act out an interview for the job.

Follow-up

12 Write out your own Curriculum Vitae, for the stage in your career you have reached now.

Now write a list of the extra items (practical work, qualifications, etc.) you would like to see on your CV *ten years from now.*

149

13 Look at the advertisements in Exercise 7, the advertisements in Exercise 11, and the advertisements below.

ASSISTANT MANAGER
FOOD & BEVERAGE

The exclusive, luxurious 112 bedroomed Athenaeum hotel situated in the heart of London's Mayfair, requires a conscientious, self-motivated professional to fulfil this challenging position in an establishment renowned for its high standards.

Duties include co-ordination, development and assistance in the management of all Food and Beverage operations. The achievement of revenue and profit targets, special responsibility for the Private Functions Department and regular duty management.

The ideal candidate will be at least 24 years of age with an HND in Hotel and Catering operation and have had sound basic training in all hotel operations, particularly Food and Beverage.

In return, we offer an excellent salary, career development opportunities and the extensive benefits you would associate with the highly successful Rank Hotels Group.

Please apply in writing with full C.V. to:

**Tony Rogers
Personnel Manager
01-499 3464**

Athenaeum Hotel

116 Piccadilly, London W1V 0BJ

✕ Rank Hotels

BVCK45-997

ROYAL HORSEGUARDS THISTLE HOTEL
2 Whitehall Court, London SW1

This 375 bedroom 4 star hotel overlooking the Thames has recently undergone refurbishment.

NIGHT MANAGER

We are seeking a professional and formally qualified person, aged 24 + with a relevant Hotel Management background and possessing excellent organisation and man-management skills.

A good working knowledge of Front Office cashiering operations is essential as you will be responsible for managing our small team of night staff.

In return we offer excellent pay and conditions together with opportunities for career development.

For more details and an interview telephone Personnel on 01-839 3400.

MVCK45-995

where individuality counts

THISTLE HOTELS

QUEEN ELIZABETH 2

Applications are invited for the positions of:

Assistant Restaurant Managers
Silver Service Waiters
Commis Waiters & Sommeliers

To work aboard the World's most prestigious Superliner, Queen Elizabeth 2.

Successful candidates should be qualified individuals who have gained a minimum of two years' experience in luxury hotels or restaurants, possess an excellent command of the English language and are seeking to secure a career within a quality working environment.

In return you can look forward to joining a successful team of enthusiastic professionals on board QE2 in positions which offer competitive salaries at every level.

If you feel that you qualify and have a sincere interest please forward your letter of application with curriculum vitae complete with recent photograph and reference papers to:

**Logbridge Ltd., 1st Floor, Unit One
City Commerce Centre, Marsh Lane
Southampton SO1 1EW**

OVCX45-229

RECEPTIONIST/ GENERAL ASSISTANT

With a bright personality, energy and flair to assist proprietor in creating a relaxed atmosphere, at the same time maintaining high standards of service in our 3 star, 30 bedroom hotel and leisure centre.

You should be experienced in all reception duties, bar, dining room, and front of house. (The position does not involve the kitchen area.)

Apply in writing or telephone Mrs Lane for an application form.

**The Court Hotel
Lamphey, Pembroke SA71 5NT
Telephone: 0646-672273**

BVCL45-937

Choose *one* of these advertisements and write a letter of application for the job.

If possible, find a partner, or a group of other students who will act as a management 'panel' and 'interview' you for the job. Give them your letter of application and CV and attend the 'interview'. Be ready to ask questions about the job yourself. At the end of the interview they should decide whether or not to offer you the job. (Note: Other students watching the interview can try to judge both the quality of the candidate and the quality of the interview. How well have the interviewers done their job?)

14 Work with a partner.

Student A
You are a hotel manager. You need staff to fill certain posts in your hotel. Write an 'advertisement' for one or more posts in your hotel. Put it in a 'magazine' (your class notice board, or pass it round your class). Find someone who wishes to 'reply' to your advertisement. 'Interview' the person, and decide whether or not to offer him/her the job.

Student B
You see student A's advertisement. Send Student A a letter of application and CV. Attend an 'interview' with Student A. Be ready to ask questions during the interview, and decide whether you want the job if you are offered it.

Language reference

Language of career description
My first job was ...
Before I got my present job I ...
After I left school I ...
I've been with ... for ... years
I took a course in ...
I worked as (a receptionist, etc.)
My ambition is to ...

General enquiries about careers using Present Perfect
How long have you been with ...
Have you taken any courses in ...?
Have you got any diplomas or certificates?
What positions have you held?
Have you worked in ... (any large hotels, etc.)?

Questions about ambitions

How do you see your career developing?
How do you see your future now?
What do you see yourself doing in the future?

Language of CVs

Name, date and place of birth; marital status; nationality; education;
qualifications; practical experience; languages; certificate; diploma;
married; single; curriculum vitae; resumé

Language of job interviews

Why do you want to (work here, etc.)?
What experience have you had of ...?
What are the main things (a receptionist should keep in mind, etc.)?
Is there anything else you want to ask?
When could you start?

Miscellaneous vocabulary

ambition	mother tongue
catering	notice (two months' notice etc.)
course	position (= job)
day release course	post
dual nationality	promote
enclosure	promotion
fluent	recommendation
general assistant	recruit
hospitality	satisfactory
hotel chain	sponsor
hotel industry	starting salary
interview	take/do a course
interview panel	trainee
managerial	

Transcript of recordings for Units 1 – 17

Unit 1: Hotel types and hotel activities

Exercise 7

Number 1
MAN: I'd like you to book me a hotel.
CLERK: Yes sir. What kind of hotel did you have in mind?
MAN: The best hotel in town. My wife has never been in England before and I want this to be the holiday of a lifetime.

Number 2
CLERK: Good morning madam.
WOMAN: Hello, I'm looking for a place to stay tonight ... somewhere not too expensive ... just Bed and Breakfast for me and the children.

Number 3
MAN: I'm passing through on business, and I need somewhere to stay for a few nights. I'd prefer a hotel in the centre of town.
CLERK: Yes sir — there's a hotel very near here where a lot of businessmen stay ... just next to the Town Hall ... It's called ...

Number 4
WOMAN: Can you recommend a nice hotel where we can stay for a week in the summer ... somewhere traditional ... on the sea front?
CLERK: Somewhere traditional ... and with a view of the sea ...
WOMAN: That's right ... you know, somewhere nice for a week's holiday ... so that we can walk along the beach whenever we want a bit of exercise ...

Number 5
MAN: We'd like somewhere outside town ... somewhere quiet ... with nice places for walking.
CLERK: Mm ... there are some nice hotels in the Weston Hills ... I've got a brochure for one here. It's a lovely, peaceful place ... it's called ...

Exercise 9

GEORGIO: Tim, let me put you in the picture about today. We have an important guest coming from the airport at half past nine — Prince Abdulkadr of Saudi Arabia.

153

TIM: A prince, eh?

GEORGIO: Yes — let me know the moment he arrives. I'll have to welcome him personally. Then at ten o'clock we have the opening of the flower exhibition.

TIM: Ten o'clock. That'll be in the Exhibition Hall, won't it?

GEORGIO: That's right. Now, at a quarter past ten we have a large wedding party starting in the main reception room.

TIM: OK ... ten fifteen ... reception room ...

GEORGIO: Then at eleven o'clock the Lions Club are holding their monthly meeting ... we'll give them the Amazon Bar and they can stay as long as they like ...

TIM: OK. I've got that ...

GEORGIO: Now, in the afternoon, we have a large group from Seagull Tours arriving at two o'clock ...

TIM: Shall I put them all on the third floor?

GEORGIO: Yes, do that. Now, from three till six, we have the Rio Bridge Club. They're meeting in the upstairs lounge ... and that's everything ... except for the Brightlights Cabaret tonight from ten till half past twelve, down in the disco.

Unit 2: Hotel staff

Exercise 4

STUDENT: So you are the person who's in overall charge of the hotel?

MANAGER: That's right. But in fact the Assistant Manager is responsible for the day-to-day running of the hotel. You see, most of my time is taken up with negotiation with travel agencies, planning, meetings, that kind of thing.

STUDENT: I see. And then, under the Assistant Manager there are all the departments of the hotel ...

MANAGER: Yes. You'll find much the same departments in every hotel, but the actual details of organization always differ somewhat. In our case we have three main divisions — the restaurant staff, the housekeeping staff, and the reception staff. Reception is what the public see. And in our case we have three receptionists who work under the Head Receptionist.

STUDENT: And do the porters come under reception too?

MANAGER: In this hotel, yes. Here, the Head Porter reports to the Head Receptionist. And the Head Porter in turn has two porters under him.

STUDENT: And housekeeping is a separate department?

MANAGER: That's right. The Head Housekeeper is in charge of the chambermaids and the cleaners.

STUDENT: What about the bars? Where do they fit in?

MANAGER: Well, we have four bar operatives looking after the bars in the hotel. But the bars and the restaurants all come under the responsibility of the Restaurant Manager. The restaurant section includes both restaurant and bar service.

STUDENT: I see. And under the Restaurant Manager you also have the waiters and the kitchen staff?

MANAGER: Yes. As regards the waiters, the Head Waiter supervises three Station Waiters and a part-time waiter. And then there are the chefs. Under the Head Chef we have the Second Chef and two trainee chefs. And there are several part-time kitchen assistants — the numbers vary.

Exercise 8

GUEST 1: Would it be possible for the hotel to get us tickets for a show tomorrow night?

GUEST 2: I have some very heavy luggage in my room. Can someone help me with it?

GUEST 3: I'm afraid I've knocked over a plate of food in my room. Could someone possibly come up and help me clear up the mess?

GUEST 4: Look, I asked for a telephone call to be put through to Paris two hours ago and I haven't heard anything since. Can't you hurry things up a bit?

GUEST 5: I've an important meeting tomorrow and I'll have to wear this suit. It needs pressing. Is there anyone here who can do that?

GUEST 6: Can you send someone up here quickly? The air conditioning is making a terrible noise, and there's water dripping from it onto the floor.

GUEST 7: This key says room 717. Is that on the seventh floor? I'll need to use the lift, won't I?

GUEST 8: I'd like to check out, and I'm in a bit of a hurry. Is the bill ready?

Stop the tape. Do not listen to the next exercise until you have tried to write in the names of the staff in Exercise 8.

Exercise 9

Now listen to the complete conversations. Fill in the sentences

GUEST 1: Would it be possible for the hotel to get us tickets for a show tomorrow night?

RECEPTIONIST: If you talk to the Head Porter he'll order tickets for you.

GUEST 2: I have some very heavy luggage in my room. Can someone help me with it?

RECEPTIONIST: No problem, sir. The porter will carry it down for you.

GUEST 3: I'm afraid I've knocked over a plate of food in my room. Could someone possibly come and help clear up the mess?

RECEPTIONIST: Certainly madam. I'll talk to the Housekeeper and she'll send someone up.

GUEST 4: Look, I asked for a telephone call to be put through to Paris two hours ago, and I haven't heard anything since. Can't you hurry things up a bit?

RECEPTIONIST: I'm sorry about that, sir. I'll contact the Switchboard Operator at once and find out the reason for the delay.

GUEST 5: I've an important meeting tomorrow and I'll have to wear this suit. It needs pressing. Is there anyone here who can do that?

RECEPTIONIST: We'll soon arrange that for you, sir. The Valet will attend to it any time you want.

GUEST 6: Can you send someone up here quickly? The air conditioning is making a terrible noise, and there's water dripping from it onto the floor.

RECEPTIONIST: I'm terribly sorry, madam. I'll call the Maintenance Engineer at once. He'll soon put it right.

GUEST 7: This key says room 717. Is that on the seventh floor? I'll need to use the lift, won't I?

RECEPTIONIST: Yes sir. The lift boy over there will take you up to the room.

GUEST 8: I'd like to check out, and I'm in a bit of a hurry. Is the bill ready?

RECEPTIONIST: If you'd like to sit down a moment, I'll tell the Cashier. He'll make up the bill immediately.

3: Room types

Exercise 5

SEC: If the terms are favourable, we could come to an arrangement for regular accommodation. Now, I wanted to discuss the types of room with you, and rates for their use.

MANAGER: Certainly. The rates I'll quote to you first of all are what we call 'rack rates', that is the normal rates quoted to the public. But obviously we would discuss a discount rate for you. Now, as regards the rooms, they are all of a very high standard. All our rooms have central heating. Most of them are with bathroom, and they all have a washbasin and a toilet.

SEC: That sounds fine. Can you tell me about your single rooms?

MANAGER: Yes. Our single rooms are very comfortable, and the rates are very reasonable. I think you'd find them suitable for visiting staff of all grades. The rack rate is £40 a night.

SEC: £40 a night ...

MANAGER: Yes. Or for real economy, let's suppose you have a sales conference. You could double up your sales staff and put them into twin rooms. That would work out very cheaply. The normal rate is £55 per twin or double room per night.

SEC: Well, we might consider that possibility. But we also have some quite important visitors sometimes. Have you any really special accommodation we can offer them?

MANAGER: Well, suppose you have visiting managerial staff. For something more luxurious, we can offer our Delphos Suite. It's delightful, and convenient for entertaining private guests. It has its own private terrace where guests can sit outside and enjoy the view over the lake ...

SEC: That sounds most attractive ...

MANAGER: The normal rate is £150 per night ...

SEC: £150.

MANAGER: ... but for total luxury, the finest accommodation of any hotel in this area, I can recommend our Bella Vista Penthouse. From the balcony, there's a magnificent view over the whole countryside.

SEC: Oh, lovely.

MANAGER: It has a bedroom connecting to a large sitting room, with a separate study, a bathroom, and a fully-fitted kitchen. It combines total luxury with total privacy. For example, if your Company Director and his wife wanted to stay for a few days it would be ideal.

SEC: And the rate?

MANAGER: The normal rate would be £220 a night.

Exercise 9

Enquiry 1

WOMAN: I'd like to book a room for myself, my husband, and our two children aged twelve and ten. Have you anything suitable?

Enquiry 2

MAN: Good morning. I'm from Melton Scientific Instruments and we're looking for a place to show some of our products and to meet possible customers. Second week of April this year. Have you got any suitable rooms?

Enquiry 3

MAN: Perhaps you've heard that Rob Nelson the pop singer is giving a concert here. I'm arranging accommodation for him. Nothing but the best will do for him — he can afford it — but you know, he doesn't want newspapermen waiting outside his door, so complete privacy is essential.

Enquiry 4

WOMAN: I'm the secretary to Sir Henry and Lady Lucas-Smith. Their daughter is twenty-one this year, and they're looking for a place to hold a small party and dance ... just one or two hundred guests ...

Enquiry 5

MAN: I'm organizing this year's meeting of the British Insurance Agents' Association, and we want to find out about the possibilities for holding it in your region. There would be two hundred to two hundred and fifty delegates and several important visiting speakers.

Now stop the tape. Do not go on to the exercise until you have finished Exercise 9.

Exercise 10

Suggestion 1

RECEPTIONIST: For that kind of occasion it would be best to use at least two rooms, including the ballroom and the adjoining reception room.

Suggestion 2

RECEPTIONIST: We have a penthouse suite that he would find ideal, sir. It's extremely luxurious, and it's well away from the public eye.

Suggestion 3

RECEPTIONIST: Would you like me to book you a family room madam? It has four comfortable beds and it's extremely spacious.

Suggestion 4

RECEPTIONIST: Well, our conference hall is specially built for that type of meeting. It will accommodate up to 300 delegates. Would you like to see it?

Suggestion 5

RECEPTIONIST: It sounds as if you would find our Exhibition Room suitable. We have a display of video equipment there at the moment. I'll get someone to show you the facilities.

Unit 4: Room furnishings and equipment

Exercise 4

GUEST 1: Can you send someone up, please? The bulb in my bedside lamp is broken.

GUEST 2: Can you help me, please? I'd like to make some telephone calls, but there's no telephone directory in this room.

GUEST 3: Can you send a chambermaid to room 303? The bedsheets haven't been changed.

GUEST 4: Hello, I'm in room 217. Does nobody look after the plants here? The plant in my room is almost dead.

GUEST 5: I'm not satisfied with this room. The carpet is very dusty.

GUEST 6: You haven't finished this room yet, have you? The ashtray needs emptying.

GUEST 7: I've just unpacked and there's a small problem in my room. There are no coathangers in the wardrobe.

GUEST 8: I'm afraid the chambermaid hasn't done a very thorough job in my room. The bath hasn't been cleaned.

Stop the tape. Do not listen to the replies to the guests until you have finished Exercise 4.

Exercise 5

Listen to the replies to the guests in Exercise 4. The replies are in a different order from the guests. Match the replies with Guests 1–8.

Reply A
Oh, I'm sorry. I didn't notice that. I'll empty it for you.

Reply B
Really? I'm very sorry about that. Some of our staff are still going through training, you see. I'll make sure she comes back and cleans it right away.

Reply C
I'm very sorry. There ought to be one in every room. I'll bring one up to your room immediately.

Reply D
Certainly, sir. The Housekeeper will be up to replace it right away.

Reply E
I'm very sorry, madam. The chambermaid should have changed them. I'll tell the Housekeeper to come up and change them now.

Reply F
Thank you for mentioning it, madam. The Housekeeper is usually very careful about watering them, but she's been on holiday this week. I'll send someone up to water it now.

Reply G
Sorry about that, sir. I'll ask the floor maid to vacuum it at once.

Reply H
Oh dear, I don't know how that could have happened. Somebody must have taken them. I'll bring some up to your room right away.

Exercise 8

Number 1
TRAINEE: In Room 101 there's a bad cigarette burn on the bedside table — a new one I think. And the bulb in the bathroom shaving lamp has gone.
FLOOR MAID: Have you replaced the bulb?
TRAINEE: Yes, I have. But what do we do about the cigarette burn?
FLOOR MAID: I'll come and see how bad the damage is.

Number 2
FLOOR MAID: What's 201 like?
TRAINEE: The TV set isn't working. I've already contacted the Maintenance Engineer.
FLOOR MAID: That's fine. Anything else?
TRAINEE: The telephone directory is badly torn.
FLOOR MAID: Oh well, you'd better replace it. You'll get one in the bookstore.

Number 3
TRAINEE: I've just come from 301 and it's in a terrible mess. They've drawn pictures on the walls, they've torn the curtains, they've broken a mirror and I think they've stolen the bedspreads ...
FLOOR MAID: We'll have to report this to the General Manager immediately. It could be a matter for the police.

Number 4
TRAINEE: There's a faulty radio in 401. It makes a terrible noise when I switch it on.
FLOOR MAID: OK. Have you reported it to the Maintenance Engineer?

TRAINEE: No, not yet.

FLOOR MAID: Well, you'd better do that now. Is the room OK otherwise?

TRAINEE: The bath is badly stained. I suppose there's rust in the pipes and it leaves a mark.

FLOOR MAID: Yes, it's a common problem here. Have you cleaned it?

TRAINEE: Not yet, but I'm going to clean it now.

Unit 5: Room rates

Exercise 3

CLERK: ... so here's a brochure with the hotels in Midford. It gives you all the rates ...

TOURIST: I'm sorry, my English isn't so good. Can you explain this to me?

CLERK: Yes, of course. First of all we have the Castle Inn ... here ... it's the cheapest. It will cost you only £12 for a single room and £15 for a double. The price includes continental breakfast. If you want a full English breakfast you'll have to pay extra ...

TOURIST: What is this 'English breakfast'?

CLERK: Oh, you know, hot food, fried egg, fried bacon, porridge ... whereas the continental breakfast is coffee, tea, rolls, jam and honey — nothing cooked, you see.

TOURIST: I think I would prefer the continental breakfast.

CLERK: Well, yes, that's included. And then we have the Dalton Hotel, more expensive, but very nice, a bathroom attached to every room. The Dalton charges £30 for a single room and £60 for a double. But there is no charge for children under 12 who stay in the same room as their parents.

TOURIST: I won't have my children with me. But maybe my husband will come a little later ...

CLERK: Well, the Park Hotel is very reasonably priced. £16 per person. Every room has a bath. There's a special rate of £25 which includes dinner, bed and breakfast — what we call half-board. Or you can have full-board, that's the room plus all meals for £29 per person per night.

TOURIST: We would only want breakfast.

CLERK: I see. Mm ... you could try the fourth hotel here, the Phoenix. It will cost you £28 for a double room with bath. Breakfast is £5 per person.

TOURIST: Yes. But what about the extra money, what do you call it in English, the service ...

CLERK: All these rates include a service charge of ten per cent. They also include VAT — that's Value Added Tax.

TOURIST: If we come later in the year will it be cheaper?

CLERK: Yes. These are the rates for June to September. You would pay less at other times of the year.

TOURIST: I'll talk about it with my husband. Thank you for explaining everything to me.

CLERK: You're very welcome.

Exercise 6

SEC: ... so we have trainees from abroad with us for several weeks at a time, and we are considering putting them with local hotels as long-stay guests.

MANAGER: Well, in that case we would charge you on a weekly basis. But of course we might be able to offer you a discount. Our most basic plan is for the room only, with no meals at all included — what we call European Plan. Our normal weekly rate for room only is £150.

SEC: £150 ... I see. But I think we would prefer to have the accommodation on the basis of meals provided — perhaps even all meals during Christmas holidays and so on ...

MANAGER: Right. We we can offer a choice of plans for this. Obviously there's the ordinary bed and breakfast system, what we call Continental Plan, and for that we normally charge £165 a week.

SEC: Just a moment. £165 ... bed and breakfast. Now, what about people who want to stay ... er ... en pension, with all meals included?

MANAGER: Well, we call that our American Plan. Our normal rate is very reasonable, really — £220 a week.

SEC: £220 ... I see. And that just leaves the trainees who have lunch in our canteen but get all their other meals in the hotel. Do you have a plan to cover this — demi-pension, including an evening meal?

MANAGER: Yes, we can certainly offer that. It's what we call our Modified American Plan. It includes room, breakfast and dinner, and the normal rate is £195 a week.

SEC: Fine. Now let me tell you more about our numbers and you can tell me what kind of discounts you can offer ...

Unit 6: Hotel reservations (1) By telephone and face to face

Exercise 4

CUSTOMER: I'd like to reserve a room for Wednesday the twenty third of April, please.

CLERK: Yes madam. For how many?

CUSTOMER: For two adults. A double room with bathroom if possible, please.

CLERK: Double room with bathroom. And how many nights are you planning to stay, madam?

CUSTOMER: Two nights — that's the nights of the twenty third and twenty fourth of April.

CLERK: Fine. We have a double room available with bathroom en suite. The rate is A$140 a night including breakfast. Would that be suitable?

CUSTOMER: Yes, that would be fine.

CLERK: And the name, please?

CUSTOMER: Simons — Mrs Mary Simons.

CLERK: Thank you. And do you know what time you'll be arriving, madam?

CUSTOMER: Oh, around half past seven, I expect.

CLERK: That's fine, madam. Thank you very much. We look forward to seeing you.

Exercises 9 & 10

Dialogue 1

CUSTOMER: Have you got a room for tonight?

CLERK: Yes sir. Single room is it?

CUSTOMER: Yes. Your cheapest single room with bathroom.

CLERK: Yes. And for how long, sir?

CUSTOMER: Just one night.

CLERK: Fine. Our cheapest single room with bathroom costs £30 including breakfast, service and VAT. Would that suit you?

CUSTOMER: Yes, that'll be fine.

CLERK: And your name is ...?

CUSTOMER: Heinrich Schwartz.

CLERK: That's fine, Mr Schwartz. The room number is 217. If you wouldn't mind filling this form in ...

Dialogue 2

CUSTOMER: Can I reserve a room for the day after tomorrow, please.

CLERK: Yes sir. Single, double or twin?

CUSTOMER: Oh, er ... twin room, please.

CLERK: With bathroom or without?

CUSTOMER: Is there much difference in price?

CLERK: Well, it's US$100 per night without bathroom and US$120 with bathroom en suite.

CUSTOMER: With bathroom then, please.

CLERK: And how many nights would you be staying?

CUSTOMER: Four nights.

CLERK: Very good sir. That's a twin room with bathroom for four nights from July 24th to 29th. And what was the name, please?

CUSTOMER: Mr and Mrs McPherson.

CLERK: And have you any idea when you'd be arriving, sir?

CUSTOMER: Quite late ... perhaps about half past nine.

CLERK: Very good, Mr McPherson. I've reserved the room for you. We look forward to seeing you tomorrow night.

Dialogue 3

CUSTOMER: Hello. I'd like to reserve a room for two adults and a child for Tuesday the fourth of September.

CLERK: Tuesday the fourth of September ... two adults and a child ... and how long would you be staying?

CUSTOMER: For two nights.

CLERK: We could give you a twin room and put an extra bed in it. Would that be suitable?

CUSTOMER: What would the charge be?

CLERK: How old is the child?

CUSTOMER: He's ten.

CLERK: Well, there would be no charge for the child. Including breakfast, the charge would be £45 per night.

CUSTOMER: That's OK then.

CLERK: Very good, sir. And could I have your name, please.

CUSTOMER: The name is Black — David Black and family.

CLERK: That's fine, Mr Black. I've reserved a room for you for two nights, the fourth and fifth of September.

Unit 7: Hotel reservations (2) Telexes and letters

Exercise 6

Number 1

Send a telex to Scantours of Copenhagen. Tell them we confirm their reservation of ten twin rooms with bath for the fourteenth to the eighteenth of August, four nights, continental plan, at the rates we agreed. Ask them to advise us of the time of arrival and send our regards.

Number 2
Now, secondly, a telex has to go to Signor Fabri of Milan Travel. Say good morning to him from Weston. Ask him if he can confirm that he is arriving on May the fifth as planned. Say we have reserved a suite for him. Say that if he advises us of his time of arrival I will meet him at the airport.

Number 3
You'd better send a telex to the Milton Hotel in Edinburgh. Ask them to reserve three single rooms with bath for three of our guests tomorow, staying for one night, the third to the fourth of September. They'll arrive at half past seven approximately. Tell them please to confirm and give us their rates. Thank them from us.

Number 4
There's also a telex for Compass Engineering. Tell them that as requested we have reserved two suites for their directors arriving on the tenth of November and leaving on the twelfth, and that the rate is £100 per person per day.

Number 5
Finally, send a telex to Signal Congress Operators in New York. Tell them that we regret that we are unable to provide the ten twin-bedded rooms they request. Say that we have reserved five twin-bedded rooms and ten singles at no extra cost. Ask them to confirm as soon as possible if this is acceptable.

Exercise 9

SECRETARY: After the expansion of the company last year, we are getting far more visitors coming over, so we would like to reserve some accommodation for some important clients of ours ... we wanted to know what you could provide ...

MANAGER: Well, that's part of our service — to work with companies and give VIP guests special treatment when necessary. So if you'll just give me the details of numbers, dates and so on, we can try to work out a package.

SECRETARY: Right then. Well, the clients concerned are three directors from Deutschland Chemicals. We would like them to have three luxury rooms with all facilities.

MANAGER: Right, I get the picture ... and as regards meals?

SECRETARY: Breakfast, of course, but any other meals would be charged to us in addition to what we agree now. However, we would like to include in the package a special dinner when they arrive — dinner for six, including the directors of our company. And we would also like some extra luxuries for them on arrival — a bottle of champagne and a bouquet of flowers in each room.

MANAGER: Yes no problem. That's included in our standard VIP package. Now the dates?

SECRETARY: The first week of July, from the first of July to the fifth of July.

MANAGER: That's four nights. Now, that's a busy time for us, and our rates would normally be high. However, I could accommodate the clients in three luxury suites, which I'll show you in a moment. For three people staying four nights, with breakfast, dinner for six on arrival and our special VIP package I can quote you a special all-inclusive rate of £1000. Of course any additional meals, drinks, etc. would be charged to you as an extra. Does that sound acceptable to you?

SECRETARY: That sounds in line with what we expected. Now, perhaps we can go into the precise details of the package and I'll look at the facilities. Then later you can confirm your terms in writing and we'll look at them and give you our written acceptance if everything is satisfactory. But I don't expect any problems on this ...

Unit 8: Hotel records (1) Reservations

Exercise 4

VOICE: Listen to the first part of the lecture.
TRAINER: Today I'm going to talk about some of the traditional ways of recording reservations. Of course some hotels use computers nowadays, but one thing is the same for almost all hotels, and that is that when the guest makes a reservation, the details of the reservation are written down on a piece of paper — that's *before* we enter the information into any other record, and *before* we key it into a computer, or anything else. The reservation is noted down.

How do we do this? Well in most hotels, you would find a *standard reservation form.* As soon as a guest makes a reservation, we write the details on the reservation form. Now, you can see an example of a reservation form on the page in front of you. A reservation form is useful in several ways. First of all it acts as a check-list. It helps you to make sure that you get *all* the necessary information from the person. Secondly, it *standardizes* the information. It gives the information in the same place and the same order for every guest, and that means we can find the information very quickly when we want it. And thirdly, it reminds us to tell the guest certain things — things he should know, like the rate for the room.

OK, so we've filled in the reservation form. Next, we can enter all the reservations into a *reservation diary* under the date when the guests are due to *arrive* ... under the date of arrival. And once again, we have an example of a page from a reservation diary for you to look at. Of course this is a loose-leaf diary, you can take pages out and put them in as you want. So you have a new page for each day of arrival. Each new page goes at the back of the diary, and each old page is removed from the front, after the guests for that day have arrived. Of course each page may have the names of several arriving guests, as you see in the example ... remember that these names *aren't* in alphabetical order. They are written down in the order in which they make their reservation.

OK, the diary is fine for checking for arrivals, but it doesn't tell at a glance which of your rooms are going to be occupied and for how long. It's useful to know the advance occupation of each room, especially in hotels with many different types of room. So we record the advance reservations on a *reservations chart.* There's an example of a reservations chart for you to look at too ... can you see it? It's useful when there are many different types of room because you can see immediately which type of room is available and match each room with the guest's requirements. And of course it's also useful in hotels where guests stay quite a long time, I mean three nights or more. Without a chart you may not easily see when the room will become available. So it is often used in the older, resort type of hotel, where guests often stay for several days and book a long time in advance.
VOICE: Stop the tape. Do not go on with the next part of the lecture until you have completed Exercise 4.

Exercise 5

VOICE: Listen to the next part of the lecture.
TRAINER: Now, none of these records we've talked about so far will let you check through

163

the names of guests alphabetically. So I'm going to deal with one type of record which lets you do this. It's a *reservation rack*, and it uses a system called the *Whitney System*. You can see a diagram of a reservation rack on the page in front of you. Now, this system is rather like a reservation diary ... but instead of putting the reservations in a diary, you write them on a special slip of paper. You can see what information goes on the slip if you look at the lower part of the diagram. The information on the top of each slip is the most important information, and that is the date of arrival, the name, and the room type required. OK, as I say, you don't have this information in a diary, but you put it on a slip, and you put the slips into a rack. All the slips for a particular arrival date are put together, in a particular place in the rack, and *within* each date they are arranged alphabetically. So you can check very quickly to see if a guest has a reservation.

Exercises 7 & 8

Number 1 (This call is made on the twenty eighth of June)
MAN: Good morning. I'd like to make a reservation from the eighth of July to the twelfth of July.
CLERK: Yes sir ... what kind of room would you like?
MAN: Oh, a single room.
CLERK: With bathroom, sir? The rate is £40 a night with bathroom and £30 without.
MAN: Oh, without bathroom will do.
CLERK: And the name is ...?
MAN: The name is Nixon — William Nixon.
Number 2 (This call is made on the fourth of July)
WOMAN: My name is Stone — Miss Betty Stone, and I'd like to book a room from the eighth to the tenth of July — that's two nights only.
CLERK: Very good, madam. Is that a single room?
WOMAN: No, a twin room with bathroom, if you have one. I'll be arriving with my sister, Miss Lilian Stone.
CLERK: Yes ... so that's a twin room with bathroom from the eighth to the tenth. And ... er ... the rate for the room is £55 a night.
WOMAN: Yes, well, that's OK.
Number 3 (This call is made on the thirtieth of June)
MAN: Have you got a room for the whole of the second week in July? A single room with a bath?
CLERK: The second week in July. Let me see ... I'm sorry sir, I'm afraid a single room with bath would only be available from the eighth to the twelfth. Would that be any use to you? The rate is £40 a night.
MAN: Yes ... yes, I think that would probably be long enough for me.
CLERK: Very good, sir. Could I have your name, please?
MAN: The name is John Bird.
CLERK: That's fine then Mr Bird. I've made a note of your reservation, single room with bath, from the eighth to the twelfth of July.
Number 4 (This call is made on the seventh of July)
MAN: I was wondering if you would have a room for tomorrow night for me and the wife.
CLERK: Tomorrow night ... that's the eighth of July. We have a nice double room with bathroom en suite. Would that be suitable? The rate is £55 a night.
MAN: Yes, that would be fine.
CLERK: And how long would you be staying, sir?

MAN: Oh, we'd be staying till the eleventh — that's three nights.
CLERK: Very good, sir. And the name?
MAN: The name is Peters ... Mr and Mrs J. Peters.
CLERK: Thank you. And do you know what time you'll be arriving?
MAN: Well, we've quite a long way to drive. We may not arrive till around 9 o'clock at night. Is that OK?
CLERK: Yes, that's fine sir — so long as we know .... I'll just make a note of it ... arriving 9 o'clock ...

Unit 9: Hotel records (2) Check-in and after

Exercise 4

GUEST: Can you help me with this form, please? My English isn't very good.
CLERK: Yes, of course sir ... let's see ... yes .... The first thing is your family name .... What's your family name, please?
GUEST: Ah, my family name. Yes, it's Benmelouka.
CLERK: Benmelouka. How do you spell that?
GUEST: B–E–N–M–E–L–O–U–K–A.
CLERK: Thank you ... and your other names? Your first names?
GUEST: It's, er ... Mohammed Hussein.
CLERK: Mohammed ... Hussein ... thank you ... and ... er ... your nationality ... er ... what country do you come from?
GUEST: I come from Morocco.
CLERK: Morocco ... right ... and your address?
GUEST: My address is 10, Liberation Street, Rabat.
CLERK: 10, Liberation Street, Rabat. And do you know your passport number? Perhaps I could look at your passport. Thanks ... ah, here it is ... one, four, zero, zero, seven, eight ... and it was issued in Rabat ... and ... I'm just looking for the place of birth. Ah, here we are. 'Casablanca'. That's a beautiful city.
GUEST: You know Casablanca?
CLERK: I was on holiday there once .... Now, sir, your destination?
GUEST: Sorry? My destin...
CLERK: What's your next destination? Where are you going after this?
GUEST: Ah yes, my *déstination*. I'm going to Paris after this.
CLERK: Paris ... thank you ... that's fine sir. If you could just sign this at the bottom here ... thank you .... Your room number is 252. Here's your key, and the bell boy there will take your suitcases.

Exercise 9

TRAINER:
In a hotel we need to know about the status of every room — a room may be ready for occupation, or it may be occupied, or it may be vacant but not ready because the housekeeper hasn't finished with it yet. Today I'm going to talk about one system which deals with this problem and lets us know the status of any room at a glance. It's called the Whitney Rack

System, and you can see a diagram of it in your book. I'd like you to look at the diagram now, please.

Basically, what you have here is a rack for all the rooms in the hotel, with a slot in the rack for each room. You can see in the diagram the room numbers 201, 202 and so on, on the left of each slot, right? Oh, and we have arrows beside some of the numbers — that shows you the rooms with doors communicating with each other. Then in the centre of each slot you have the room types, so that for example room 204 is a double room with bath, room 205 is a double room and room 206 is a twin room with bath ... you see? So we have room numbers, and room types. But which of these rooms are ready for occupation? This is the clever part of it. How do we know if a room is ready or not?

Well, partly it's obvious. Look at the diagram again, at rooms 212 and 214. We don't have the room type there. Instead we have the names of the guests who are staying there, and their departure date ... do you see? Mr and Mrs Whitfield, and Mr and Mrs Lynch. What's happened is that the receptionist has filled in a slip of paper with their names, departure date and other information. Then she's folded the slip and slotted the slip into the rack. So rooms 212 and 214 have guests staying in them and they're not available for occupation. But what about the other rooms? Does this mean that Rooms 201 to 213 are available?

Actually it doesn't mean that. The way we show the room status for rooms 201 to 213 is by using a perspex slider — that is, a piece of plastic that you can see through and that slides over the room type. Now take for example room 209, a twin-bed room. The slider for that room is clear, it doesn't show any colour in its present position. That means that the room is vacant and that it is ready to let. You can allocate that room if a guest arrives. But now look at the room below it, room 210, a single room. The slider here is yellow. That means that the room is vacant, but it isn't ready yet — probably the chambermaid hasn't had time to get to work on it yet. So we can't allocate this room just yet. But the room below that, room 211, is different. The slider here is at the red position. That means that the room has just been let. It doesn't have a rack slip yet because there hasn't been time to write one out, but it has been let, and we can't allocate that room to another guest.

Unit 10: Using the telephone

Exercise 4

Dialogue 1
OPERATOR: Good morning, Park Hotel. May I help you?
MAN: Hello. Can I speak to Mr Conrad Schultz, please?
OPERATOR: I'm sorry, what was the name, please?
MAN: Conrad Schultz.
OPERATOR: Schultz ... er ... that's Room 209 .... Just hold the line, please. It's ringing for you now.
Dialogue 2
OPERATOR: Good morning, Park Hotel. May I help you?
WOMAN: Hello. Could you put me through to Mr Lyons, Room 113, please?
OPERATOR: Hold the line please.

OPERATOR: Still trying to connect you.

OPERATOR: It's ringing for you now.

OPERATOR: I'm sorry, I'm not getting any reply. Can I take a message?

WOMAN: Yes. Can you tell him that Mrs Beanny phoned? That's B−E−A−double N−Y. He's got my number.

OPERATOR: Thank you − that's B for Benjamin, E for Edward, A for Andrew, double N for Nellie, Y for Yellow?

WOMAN: You've got it.

OPERATOR: Thank you, Mrs Beanny. I'll give Mr Lyons the message.

Dialogue 3

OPERATOR: Good morning, Park Hotel. May I help you?

WOMAN: Hello, could I speak with Miss Brown, Room 112?

OPERATOR: Hold the line please.

OPERATOR: I'm sorry, the number is engaged. Would you like to hang on?

WOMAN: No, I don't think so. Perhaps you could tell her to call me. I'm her sister, and I'm at five zero four six eight eight.

OPERATOR: Five oh four six double eight .... Yes, I'll give her the message.

Dialogue 4

OPERATOR: Good morning, Park Hotel. May I help you?

MAN: I'd like to make a reservation, pleae.

OPERATOR: Hold on a moment, please, I'll put you through to reception.

RECEPTIONIST: Park Hotel, Reception, can I help you?

MAN: Hello, I'd like to make a reservation for the 25th of August, one night only ... a single room with bath if you have one ...

Exercise 11

CALLER 1 (The time is half past two in the afternoon)

Hello ... this is Klaus Bauer speaking .... Can I speak to Mr Tom Johnson, please? ... Oh ... perhaps you can give him a message ... tell him ... I'll call at his office around eleven thirty tomorrow morning .... Yes, eleven thirty ... the name is Bauer, that's B−A−U−E−R .... Oh, thank you very much.

CALLER 2 (The time is a quarter to eleven in the morning)

I'd like to leave a message for Miss Harding please ... no, don't bother to phone her, just give her the message ... tell her I've reached the parcel she sent me and everything is fine .... That's right, everything is fine .... My name? Oh yes, it's Mrs Hyatt ... that's H for Harry, Y for Yellow, A for Andrew, double T for Tommy. Hyatt. Yes, thank you very much.

CALLER 3 (The time is a quarter past six in the evening)

Hello, my name is Salwa Al Azabi and I'd like to speak to Mrs Forest, please .... Ah, she's not in? ... Yes, thanks, if you could tell her to phone me .... Yes, it's Miss Al Azabi ... that's Al, A−L, and then Azabi, A−Z−A−B−I .... That's right ... and my phone number is oh one, two seven nine, three eight double-six. Yes, three, eight, double-six. That's it ... thank you.

CALLER 4 (The time is nine o'clock at night)

My name is Robert Lett, can I speak to Mr Waddell ... No, Waddell ... W−A−double D−E−double L .... Yes, it's a terrible line isn't it? He's not staying in the hotel? But he told me .... Back tomorrow night you say? OK, if you could tell him I'd like to arrange a meeting with him .... Yes, Robert Lett, L−E−double T .... Tell him I'll phone him tomorrow night around ten o'clock .... Yes, I hope I catch him then. Thank you. Goodnight.

167

Unit 11: Hotel services (1) General services

Exercise 3

Dialogue 1
GUEST: Where can I park my car?
CLERK: You can park your car in the car park behind the hotel. It's free. Or we have a lock-up underground car park. The entrance to that is behind the hotel, too.
Dialogue 2
GUEST: I don't have a car and I'm not sure how I can get to the airport tomorrow morning.
CLERK: There's no problem about transport to the airport. We have a courtesy coach to the airport that leaves every half-hour. It only takes ten minutes to get there.
Dialogue 3
GUEST: Is there a laundry service in the hotel?
CLERK: Yes indeed sir. Just leave your laundry bag behind the door with a laundry slip in it before nine o'clock. Your laundry will be collected and returned to you by six o'clock in the evening.
Dialogue 4
GUEST: Is it possible to send a telex from here?
CLERK: Certainly sir. You can hand in a telex here at the reception desk, and we'll send it off for you. Our telex number is PARK3042, if you need it.
Dialogue 5
GUEST: I've got some valuable jewellery with me. I'd better not leave it in my room, had I?
CLERK: That's right madam. The hotel will not take responsibility for valuables left in a room. But jewellery can be deposited in one of our safe-deposit boxes here at reception, and the hotel will then be responsible for its security.
Dialogue 6
GUEST: I won't be back in the hotel till after midnight tonight. Will it be possible to get something to eat in my room?
CLERK: Certainly madam. Just dial 4 from your room and tell Room Service what you'd like. Hot and cold snacks are available at any time of the day or night.

Exercise 7

MARTIN: One thing we ought to have is a baby-listening service with a microphone in each room. I know the hotel provides a baby-sitting service with someone staying in the room, if guests specially want it. But we should offer a listening service from the central switchboard as well.
ALFRED: Well we'll have to find out the possibilities. The thing that strikes me as most important is that we should modernize our telephone system. At present we only have direct-dialling for local calls — long distance calls have to go through the switchboard operator. There ought to be modern equipment that would meter *all* outgoing calls, automatically. The charge would appear on the bills automatically, too.
MARTIN: That's right. Most hotels have that nowadays, and business people certainly want to be able to dial long distance calls directly.
ALFRED: Talking about business facilities, we should provide better photocopying facilities. We've been asking guests to hand in any documents for photocopying at reception. We ought to provide a photocopier with public access so that guests could do their own photocopying if they wished.

MARTIN: I agree. And we should have a photography service for passport photographs and so on. We could organize that through the Hall Porter.

ALFRED: There's another facility we don't offer at present and that's a shoe-cleaning facility — you know, shoe-cleaning machines. They're quite useful if you want a quick shoeshine. We could install one on each corridor. Things like that can make all the difference ...

Unit 12: Hotel services (2) Directions and general enquiries

Exercise 4

Enquiry 1
GUEST: How can I get to the Terrace Cafe, please?
CLERK: It's on this floor. Go right through the coffee shop and you'll see it just in front of you. It's at the far end of the coffee shop.

Enquiry 2
GUEST: Could you possibly direct me to the tennis courts, please?
CLERK: If you go outside, through the main door you'll see them on the left as you go out. They're part of the Sports Complex, next to the swimming pool.

Enquiry 3
GUEST: We're looking for the bar.
CLERK: The lobby bar is just over there, behind you, madam. Or we have the 1815 bar, over there to the right, through the foyer.

Enquiry 4
GUEST: Is this the right way for the souvenir shop?
CLERK: Yes. Just go along to the end of the corridor. You'll see it opposite the bank. It's the last shop on the right, next to the barber's.

Enquiry 5
GUEST: Can you tell me the way to the disco please?
CLERK: Just go down these stairs and follow the corridor along to your right. You'll hear the music — you can't miss it.

Exercises 9 and 10

Enquiry 1
GUEST: Would it be possible for me to get my car washed here?

Enquiry 2
GUEST: Have you got any information about the floor shows in the hotel this week?

Enquiry 3
GUEST: Is there anywhere we can buy some souvenirs?

Enquiry 4
GUEST: We'd like to get a good meal — not just a light snack. Are any of your main restaurants still open?

Enquiry 5
GUEST: Have you got any telephone directories for other areas? I'd like to find a number in Birmingham.

Enquiry 6
GUEST: Is it possible to book theatre tickets in the hotel?

Enquiry 7
GUEST: Can you tell me what time the shops close here?

Enquiry 8
GUEST: Can you tell me about your car parking facilities, please?
VOICE: Stop the tape. Do not listen to the enquiries with their replies until you have finished Exercise 9 and Exercise 10.

Exercise 11
VOICE: Now listen to the enquiries and the replies to the enquiries.
Enquiry 1
GUEST: Would it be possible for me to get my car washed here?
CLERK: Certainly sir. If you give your keys to the hall porter over there by the door he'll arrange it for you. The charge is £3.
Enquiry 2
GUEST: Have you got any information about the floor shows in the hotel this week?
CLERK: We have a different show in the hotel every night, madam. Tonight we have Layla and her belly dancers. You'll find a poster on the hotel notice board giving details of all our shows for the next two weeks.
Enquiry 3
GUEST: Is there anywhere we can buy some souvenirs?
CLERK: There's a souvenir shop along the corridor, on the right. It has a selection of souvenirs from this part of the world. It's open till eight o'clock.
Enquiry 4
GUEST: We'd like to get a good meal — not just a light snack. Are any of your main restaurants still open?
CLERK: Yes. There's the Waterloo Grill on the first floor. It closes at midnight.
Enquiry 5
GUEST: Have you got any telephone directories for other areas? I'd like to find a number in Birmingham?
CLERK: That's no problem, madam. We have telephone directories for most areas. I'll get you the directory for Birmingham.
Enquiry 6
GUEST: Is it possible to book theatre tickests in the hotel?
CLERK: Yes, you can get tickets from the travel agency, second shop from the end of the corridor. It makes bookings for all the shows. It'll be open tomorrow at nine o'clock.
Enquiry 7
GUEST: Can you tell me what time the shops close here?
CLERK: They close around five thirty most days. But there's late-night shopping till eight on Friday nights.
Enquiry 8
GUEST: Can you tell me about your car parking facilities, please?
CLERK: Well, there's the ordinary car park behind the hotel. You can park there free of charge. Or we have a lock-up underground car park. It's completely secure. The charge for that is £5 per night.

Unit 13: Hotel services (3) The hotel as a product

Exercise 4

So it's important if you work in a hotel to know as much as possible about the hotel. In some hotels the Receptionist keeps a sheet full of facts about the hotel at the reception desk.

You can see an example of a fact sheet like that in front of you. It's a photocopy, I'm afraid, so some of the words aren't very clear, but I hope you can follow it. It has examples for an imaginary hotel, the Royal George Hotel, written into it.

So we have the fact sheet, with the name of the hotel and all the other things the staff should know. You should be able to give the full postal address of the hotel, together with the telephone number and the telex number ... and the telephone number should include the area code for callers phoning from outside the area, as in the example, with the area code given here in brackets. OK? Now, often, staff don't realize that the people who run the hotel are part of the hotel 'product' too. So you should know the names of the people in charge of different departments. You should know the owner of the hotel, and the General Manager. Often the owner will actually be a company, not an individual. For example we have 'Trustee Hotels' as the owner in our fact sheet.

Now of course, rooms are very important. You should know everything a customer might ask. Obviously, you have to know the types of room, and the rates for each type of room. Here in our example we have the rooms and we have the rates beside them. Some hotels train their staff by having them stay in the rooms for the night and getting to know the rooms that way. Check-in and check-out times, you should know these too. You see in the example that the hotel expects guests who have made bookings to check in by ten at night and check out by nine thirty in the morning.

Now one very important thing to know about is transport connections. Guests will ask you how to get to the hotel. You ought to know the transport connections for the hotel — how to get to it by road, by bus or by rail. You can see in the example the road numbers and their classification, the bus line, and the nearest railway station and main line for rail travel. You should know about taxis, too, and how much the fare is likely to be.

OK, so you should know about transport connections. And you should know where guests can park their cars — if they come by car. In the example we have the heading, 'parking' and under it the two car-parking facilities — the ordinary car park, and the lock-up garage which guests pay £5 a night for.

What else about the hotel? You should know if the hotel is mentioned in any guide books — guide books like the AA guide or the RAC guide. Also how many stars it rates from any large tourist or motoring organizations — in this example we have a star rating of four stars in the AA, and three stars from the RAC.

Well these are the main points, but there's just one other thing to remember and that's any restrictions that guests must keep to. You should know about any rules that have to be followed — restrictions about payment, etc. Some hotels might not allow payment by certain credit cards, or they might demand payment in advance for certain categories of guest. In our example on the fact sheet we have the heading 'restrictions', and the example that guests must give proof of identity ... er ... such as passport or driving licence, or they must pay in advance if they are chance guests after a certain time of night — that is, if you just drop into the hotel after nine o'clock you should either prove who you are or pay for your night's stay beforehand.

Exercises 8 and 9

Extract 1
The restaurant is still open, sir, if you would care for a meal. Or you can get a snack in the Coffee Shop, or from Room Service, at any time.

Extract 2

I'm sure you would find a stay here most relaxing .... The hotel is fully centrally-heated, with a delightful view over Clearwater Lake .... It's located in on the edge of a pine forest, not far from Blue Ridge Mountains, ideal if you like walking and fishing .... You're welcome, sir.

Extract 3

Yes, certainly madam. You can use the hotel swimming pool free, at any time .... Or perhaps you would like to make use of the facilities in our new sports complex? ... They include a sauna bath with its own swimming pool, and a fully-equipped gymnasium ...

Extract 4

Yes, I can offer you a choice of rooms .... We can give you 210 with has a private bath for $75 a night, or we have 215 which is larger and has cable television for $90 a night ...

Unit 14: Check-out

Exercise 4

GUEST: I'd like to check out now, please. Room 301.

CLERK: Certainly sir, I'll get you your bill.

CLERK: Here we are. How would you like to pay, sir? Credit card?

GUEST: Yes, credit card. Do you take this card?

CLERK: We do indeed, sir. If I could just have your card a moment ...

CLERK: I'm sorry sir, but I'm afraid this credit card has expired. It expired at the beginning of this month.

GUEST: Oh dear, that's a nuisance. Could I pay by cheque, then?

CLERK: I'm afraid we wouldn't normally accept a cheque without a valid cheque guarantee card. But don't worry, we'll soon sort this out for you. If you'd like to wait a moment, we'll put a telephone call through to your bank. I expect they'll guarantee the cheque for you ...

GUEST: Actually, you won't need to do that. I've just remembered I have an American Express card as well .... Just a moment .... Yes, here it is. I think you'll find it's OK.

CLERK: Yes .... Yes, that'll do nicely sir. If you just wait a second I'll write out a slip for you, and give you a receipt ...

Exercise 11

CLERK: Here's your bill sir.

GUEST: Oh, thank you. Let's have a look at it now .... Goodness! It's a lot more than I expected.

CLERK: Would you like me to explain any items, sir?

GUEST: Just a moment ... yes ... what's this charge for £8.50 marked 'J'?

CLERK: 'J' is a charge for a long distance telephone call, sir. Did you make a telephone call that night?

GUEST: Yes! I remember now ... good heavens, we must have talked for a long time! And these ones, 'L' for £7 and here's another, £3.40, what are they for?

CLERK: 'L' is for hotel services. Perhaps you used the laundry service? Or got something from Room Service?

GUEST: Yes, you're right. I did get some laundry done. And I got some sandwiches from

Room Service .... What about these ones marked 'D' — £4.50 each. What does 'D' stand for?

CLERK: 'D' stands for breakfast ...

GUEST: Ah yes, I forgot, breakfast isn't included in the price of the room ...

CLERK: And you may find some other meals marked also ... yes ... here you have 'E' for lunch ... and 'G' for dinner.

GUEST: Oh well, I suppose the bill must be right. What's this charge? Look 30 pence, marked 'M'?

CLERK: 'M' is for the news-stand. Perhaps you bought a newspaper this morning.

GUEST: Oh yes, so I did. Oh well, I see it's correct. Thanks for explaining everything.

CLERK: You're welcome, sir.

Unit 15: Dealing with complaints

Exercise 4

WOMAN: Can't you do something about the service in this hotel?

DUTY MANAGER: I'm sorry, madam. What's the problem, exactly?

WOMAN: My breakfast, that's the problem ...!

DUTY MANAGER: Yes ...

WOMAN: I ordered breakfast from Room Service ... oh, at least half an hour ago ...

DUTY MANAGER: Yes ...

WOMAN: I've telephoned Room Service three times, but my breakfast still hasn't come ...

DUTY MANAGER: I see ...

WOMAN: ... I've got an important meeting at nine o'clock and now it seems I'll have to go there without breakfast! Really, I don't think this is good enough!

DUTY MANAGER: I'm very sorry about this, madam. You ordered breakfast half an hour ago, and you've phoned three times since then?

WOMAN: That's right.

DUTY MANAGER: I really must apologize. You should have received the breakfast no later than five or ten minutes after you ordered it.

WOMAN: That's what I thought.

DUTY MANAGER: The problem may be that they've been rather short-staffed in the kitchens recently. But I'll look into this, and I'll make sure that the breakfast is sent to you immediately. Full English breakfast, was it?

WOMAN: Full English breakfast, with corn flakes.

DUTY MANAGER: Very well, madam. I'll deal with this myself, and I'll have it sent up to your room right away.

Exercise 9

Dialogue 1

GUEST: What's the meaning of this? I asked for hotel accommodation, not a cowshed!

CLERK: Madam? What's the trouble exactly?

GUEST: The room you gave me! I've never seen such a disgusting mess.

CLERK: I'm sorry, madam. Why don't we go through to the lounge and we'll sort out the problem.

GUEST: I hope so, and fast ...

CLERK: Now, madam. I'm extremely sorry about this. You say the room is in a mess?

GUEST: It certainly is. The bed isn't made ... and the bathroom is full of water ...

CLERK: Yes.

GUEST: And the bath is filthy ... and the toilet is disgusting ...

CLERK: I see.

GUEST: And someone has spilled drinks or something over the floor.

CLERK: I see. So that's both the bathroom and the bedroom that are unsuitable for guests' use.

GUEST: Exactly.

CLERK: Well madam, as I say, I'm extremely sorry about this. There's obviously been a misunderstanding between us here at Front Office and the Housekeeping Department. We seem to have given you a room which should have been marked down for thorough cleaning. What I'm going to do now is contact the Housekeeper personally and make sure that you have a room that is fully up to standard.

GUEST: It'd better be.

CLERK: And in the meantime, perhaps you'd care for a drink, compliments of the house? Why don't you let me put an order through to the bar ...?

Dialogue 2

CLERK: And your name, sir?

GUEST: Glen ... John Glen.

CLERK: Just a moment, Mr Glen ... I'm sorry, Mr Glen. I have instructions that we cannot offer you accommodation.

GUEST: What? What's this all about?

CLERK: There's nothing further I can tell you Mr Glen. But these are the instructions, quite clearly. You are not to be admitted to the hotel.

GUEST: But ... this is ridiculous! I've been coming to this hotel for twenty years! I demand an explanation!

CLERK: I have no explanation here — just instructions that you are not to be admitted. I'm afraid I must ask you to leave.

GUEST: This is absurd! Look, young man, I must have an explanation of all this. I demand to see the Manager, at once.

Dialogue 3

GUEST: What nonsense is this? What kind of people do you employ here? I've been coming to this hotel for twenty years and I've never heard such rudeness.

MANAGER: I'm sorry about this, sir. Would you like to come through to the office at the back?

MANAGER: So I understand there's been a problem, sir ... it's Mr Glen, isn't it?

GUEST: That's right. You know me don't you? But what about your Reception clerk? He told me he couldn't allow me into the hotel! As soon as he heard my name he told me he wasn't allowed to give me a room under any circumstances!

MANAGER: Oh dear, I'm very sorry to hear about this, Mr Glen. There seems to have been a complete misunderstanding ...

GUEST: There must have been ...

MANAGER: The fact is, there was another Mr Glen who stayed in the hotel some months ago and caused us some trouble. When the clerk heard your name he obviously thought it was you ...

GUEST: Well this is ridiculous, isn't it?

MANAGER: I quite agree with you, Mr Glen. Look, I tell you what I'll do. First of all, I'll sort out this mistake with the reception clerk so that you can be sure it'll never happen again. And during your stay I invite you to stay in our luxury suite, at no extra cost. We want to show how much we value those guests who have stayed with us over the years ...

Exercise 11

Dialogue 1
MANAGER: Excuse me, madam ...
GUEST: Yes?
MANAGER: Could I speak to you a moment?
GUEST: Yes. What is it?
MANAGER: It's about your dog.
GUEST: Dog? Ah, you mean my little Fifi here ...
MANAGER: Yes madam. I understand you've been keeping it in your room.
GUEST: Of course I have. My little Fifi goes everywhere with me. Don't you my sweet? Poochie-poochie-poo ...
MANAGER: Yes, I understand madam. It's just that, unfortunately, we'll have to ask you to make other arrangements ...
GUEST: What do you mean, 'other arrangements'? Can't I have my little dog with me?
MANAGER: I'm afraid not, madam. The health regulations here don't permit guests to bring animals into hotel rooms — except for guide-dogs for the blind. I'm sorry, but we have to follow the rules.
GUEST: I think this is disgraceful!
MANAGER: Yes madam, but I'm sure you'll understand our position. If you wish, the Hall Porter will be pleased to help you to arrange kennel facilities. In fact, we have a special arrangement with a place near the hotel. I'm sure you would find it satisfactory ...

Dialogue 2
MANAGER: Excuse me gentlemen. Could I have a word with you? In my office, if you don't mind ...
GUEST 1: Yeah, what is it, mate?
MANAGER: This morning I had a report from the Housekeeper about the condition of your room. I went up to have a look at it myself. There's a lot of damage, isn't there?
GUEST 2: Yeah, well, so what? OK we had a bit of a party last night and a few little things got broken. But you can't expect us to pay for a few breakages, mate.
MANAGER: It's more than a few breakages, I would say. The window is broken and the TV set has been smashed. The bath is damaged beyond repair and someone has been painting pictures on the walls. And someone has tried to burn the blankets ...
GUEST 1: Yeah, but that's your problem, isn't it?
MANAGER: No, it isn't. Not exactly. We shall have to ask you for payment towards the re-decoration of the room and the replacement of the damaged items — otherwise we'll be forced to make this a police matter.
GUEST 2: Oh come on, you'd never do that ...
MANAGER: I'm afraid we'd be unable to avoid it. I'd also remind you that hotels have the right to retain guests' belongings in cases where guests owe money to the hotel. I'm sure you wouldn't want to be inconvenienced in this way ...

Dialogue 3
MANAGER: Good evening sir. I'm the Manager.
GUEST: Ah, good evening.
MANAGER: I'm afraid we've had a complaint about the noise from your neighbour across

the corridor. He's trying to get some sleep as he has an early start tomorrow. I'm sure you understand.

GUEST: Oh, I see,

MANAGER: Could we ask you and your friends to keep the noise down a little, do you think? We do like to give our guests a chance of getting a good night's sleep. And it is after midnight.

GUEST: Oh, I'm sorry. I suppose we were talking rather loudly. It's just that we've signed an important contract, you see. We were having a bit of a celebration.

MANAGER: I'm pleased to hear it. Shall I ask Room Service to bring you some coffee?

GUEST: No, no, it's all right. We were just going to pack up anyway.

MANAGER: Well, thank you sir, and good night to you.

Unit 16: Conference facilities

Exercise 6

MILNE: ... so the conference would be from the second to the sixth of April, with around 320 participants. Have you the facilities for that number of people on those dates?

MANAGER: Yes — these dates would be suitable. We have a Farmers' Union Conference finishing on the twenty-eighth of March, and a Lawyers' Conference starting on the tenth of April, so we can fit you in very well. As regards the facilities, perhaps I can give you a brief idea of what we can offer.

MILNE: Yes please, if you can give me some idea ...

MANAGER: Basically, we have a multi-purpose conference centre with seating for over 450 delegates — that's including the seating in the auditorium. Our main auditorium seats 350 people.

MILNE: So, good, it could hold all our delegates if we had a full session of the conference?

MANAGER: Certainly. But we also have two smaller conference rooms, each with an area of thirty-five square metres, which can be used for lectures if necessary. The smaller conference rooms have a seating capacity of about 55 each.

MILNE: I see ...

MANAGER: We have sound-proof folding doors between the conference rooms. These can be opened up to form a single large room. So you could have an extra seating capacity of about 110.

MILNE: Good, that could be a useful feature. What about the technical side? How about audiovisual facilities? At our last conference we had problems with the equipment.

MANAGER: The auditorium has built-in audiovisual equipment. We've found it performs extremely well.

MILNE: That sounds good. Now, we may have a large group of students from Newburgh University coming to hear a famous visiting speaker. Can you link the auditorium with the other rooms?

MANAGER: Yes, indeed. We can provide a closed circuit television link-up from the auditorium to the smaller conference halls.

MILNE: Good. Now, we may have several participants from Japan and China this year. Is there equipment for translation?

MANAGER: Yes, there is. Our main auditorium has full simultaneous translation equipment. And you'll find that both the auditorium and the conference rooms have excellent acoustics.

That's important when you have a lot of participants listening to a foreign language, isn't it?

MILNE: Indeed it is.

MANAGER: There's also an exhibition hall, for display purposes. You may be planning to exhibit books and equipment and it provides you with an area of 30 square metres.

MILNE: Yes, we would like some exhibition space. By the way, have you got any leaflets or brochures on these facilities? I'd like to study all the details.

MANAGER: Certainly. I'll give you a leaflet with a complete description of the facilities, and a plan of the actual conference centre. But why don't you come with me now and have a look at the complete centre? I think you'll find it quite an impressive building ...

Exercises 10 & 11

MILNE: OK, so if I just run through the equipment with you ... I see you have the overhead projector and the screen already in position. Now, how about pens?

MANAGER: We have some black pens in this box. But perhaps you'll need some extra colours.

MILNE: Yes. Perhaps you could get some extra felt-tip pens in different colours. I'm sure our speakers will need them.

MANAGER: Certainly. I'll order a complete range.

MILNE: This slide projector doesn't seem to be working. It probably needs a new bulb.

MANAGER: I'll attend to that right away. No ... it won't be necessary. It wasn't plugged in properly.

MILNE: Fine. Now, let's see. The tape recorder has an empty spool, but the film projector doesn't seem to have an empty reel.

MANAGER: No, that's in my office. The Personnel Manager borrowed it. I'll make a note of it.

MILNE: And do you have an extra cartridge for the slide projector?

MANAGER: Yes, there are two in this drawer here.

MILNE: Good. I see you have an electronic typewriter on this shelf ... and there's typing paper ... carbon paper ... and paper clips.

MANAGER: Yes, indeed, but there's still some stationery to come. My secretary will be up soon with pencils, notepads, folders and name tags. And the gavel ...

MILNE: Yes, we'll need that. Our discussions can get rather heated sometimes.

MANAGER: You'll also need a notice board. I'll make sure there's one ready for you. By the way, you'll find a box of drawing pins on this shelf where we keep the pens for the whiteboard, and the pointer.

MILNE: Ah yes, we have the whiteboard here .... Now, is there anything we've forgotten, do you think?

MANAGER: We could perhaps test out the PA system. There's nothing more annoying than finding the amplifier isn't adjusted properly or the microphone isn't connected.

MILNE: ... or if you get a horrible whine coming through the loudspeakers. Yes, you're right — we'd better test it. What about the lighting? Can you show me how it works?

MANAGER: Yes. Here's your dimmer switch for the main hall lighting and here's a switch for the spotlights. There's a lectern light on the lectern itself ... you see?

MILNE: Fine ... I think that's everything. Let's go and test this PA system.

MANAGER: Didn't you say you would need the translation equipment?

MILNE: No, we won't need it after all. We were expecting some participants from China and Japan, but they won't be coming this year.

Unit 17: Careers

Exercise 3

Interview 1

INTERVIEWER: Can you tell me how you came to choose hotel work?

UNA: Well, I became interested in hotel work because my mother is in the hotel industry. She's a housekeeper with one of the big London hotels. Then at school I was good at languages. I speak French and German. So hotel reception seemed like a good career.

INTERVIEWER: And did you go through training as a hotel receptionist?

UNA: Yes. After I left school I went to a Hotel College and did a Hotel Reception course. The Hotel Reception Certificate is useful, career-wise.

INTERVIEWER: And where did you start work?

UNA: My first job was as trainee Receptionist in the Ibex Hotel in Brighton, from 1981 to 1983.

INTERVIEWER: I see, and then you got your present job?

UNA: No. Before I got my present job as Senior Receptionist I spent two years at the Paris Grand Ibex Hotel. I did various Front Office jobs there, so it was useful experience. Then I got my present job with Birmingham Ibex.

INTERVIEWER: So you've been six years with Ibex now ...

UNA: Just over six years.

INTERVIEWER: And what about the future? How do you see your career developing?

UNA: I don't know .... Obviously I'd be hoping for a higher managerial post, perhaps Assistant Manager, not necessarily with Ibex ... but we'll have to wait and see.

Interview 2

INTERVIEWER: You've been in the hotel industry quite a long time, haven't you Ahmed?

AHMED: Yes, ten years now. But only three years with Ibex.

INTERVIEWER: Where did you work before that?

AHMED: In Alexandria. I started as a porter in a hotel in Alexandria ... right at the bottom, you could say. But I'd always wanted to do hotel work ... I'd always liked meeting people — and as you know the tradition of hospitality to guests is very important in Egypt ...

INTERVIEWER: Yes, indeed ...

AHMED: So I went to a technical school in Alexandria and got my Hotel Diploma and got that job as a porter ... that was in 1977. I must have done well, for they promoted me to Junior Receptionist the same year!

INTERVIEWER: That was quick promotion.

AHMED: Then I got a job as Receptionist in the Pyramid Hotel, Cairo. I was there for four years. It was there I met my wife — she's English ...

INTERVIEWER: Oh — no wonder your English is so good!

AHMED: Thanks. Anyway, the Cairo Ibex took me on then ... I suppose being able to speak English and French counted in my favour. That was as trainee Assistant Manager. Then we got the chance to move to Britain, and I continued my training here at the Ibex in Glasgow.

INTERVIEWER: And how do you see the future now?

AHMED: Oh, I'd definitely like to go back to Egypt and have my own hotel ... a first-class international hotel, along the coast from Alexandria.

Interview 3

INTERVIEWER: Pedro, you've just started in the hotel industry, I think?

PEDRO: Not quite true, actually. I've been in hotels all my life! You see my father owns a small hotel in Madrid ...

INTERVIEWER: Oh, I see. But you've just started with Ibex?

PEDRO: That's right — I've been there less than a year. And now I'm going through my training with them.

INTERVIEWER: But you obviously know the industry very well.

PEDRO: Well, of course, I worked for my father, doing most hotel jobs. But I still need to go through the training. That's why I'm in Britain now, to spend six months doing various front-of-house jobs.

INTERVIEWER: I must say, your English is very good.

PEDRO: English, French, Portuguese — and Spanish of course. That was one reason Ibex took me on.

INTERVIEWER: You didn't actually go to Hotel School in Spain, then?

PEDRO: In my case, no. I worked in my father's hotel for two years after I left secondary school. Then I joined Ibex. But next year I'll start day-release courses in Madrid as part of my training.

INTERVIEWER: And what do you see yourself doing in the future? What's your ambition?

PEDRO: My ambition? Oh, to own the largest chain of hotels in the world! What else!

Exercise 9

ROGERS: Good morning, Mr Husseini. Please sit down.

AHMED: Thank you.

ROGERS: Now, I see from your curriculum vitae that most of your career has been spent with the Ibex chain. Why do you want to work in a smaller, independent hotel, like this?

AHMED: I feel that with a smaller hotel there would be more face-to-face contact with people. Also, I think the work would be more varied and there would be more scope for developing new ideas.

ROGERS: I see. Now, our restaurant and banqueting is very important. What experience have you had in that line?

AHMED: Well, the Ibex in Newcastle deals with more banquets and large-scale functions than any other hotel in the North of England. A lot of my work has involved supervising that side of things.

ROGERS: I'm glad to see you speak some French as we have quite a few guests from France. *Vous n'avez jamais habité en France?*

AHMED: *Non, mais il y a beaucoup de français qui viennent en Egypte, vous savez.*

ROGERS; Good ... that sounds all right. Now tell me what would you say are the main things for an Assistant Manager of a hotel to keep in mind?

AHMED: I would say that attention to detail is very important ... making sure that every customer is treated politely and goes away satisfied. But looking after the staff well, getting on with them, seeing that they are happy too.

ROGERS: Quite. Quite. And in our hotel we have staff from several different nationalities, which sometimes makes things a bit tricky. Now, is there anything you would like to ask about the job?

AHMED: What kind of accommodation do you offer?

ROGERS: Ah yes. There's a house about a mile from the hotel. It's been recently modernized. Or there's a suite of rooms actually on the premises. But I expect as you're married ...

AHMED: Yes, it sounds as if the house would be more suitable. And then there's the question of salary.

ROGERS: Yes, of course. Well, we are offering a starting salary of £9,500 a year — plus accommodation that is, and meals during duty hours. But if we get on well we could reconsider that figure after a suitable period.

AHMED: I see.

ROGERS: Well now, I expect you'd like to have a look round. Oh yes, one thing, when could you start?

AHMED: Well, my present job requires two months' notice. So I could start any time after the end of April this year.

APPENDIX 2

Information gap
exercises for Students B and C

Unit 1, Exercise 14

Student B

You are the manager of the hotel. You have made certain arrangements without telling your secretary, as follows:

09.30: You are meeting Mr Dexter, a tour operator for Seagull Tours. The meeting may last most of the morning.
12.30: You want to catch a plane to go the the National Hotel Conference. You plan to come back tomorrow, and you hope that your Assistant Manager will take care of things while you are away.

Discuss the events of the day with your secretary, and decide if any changes of plan will be necessary. You can talk about your decisions like this:

I'll go later/change the time of the meeting/postpone the meeting till later/ask someone to do something ..., etc.
I'll/We'll have to meet someone/have a change of plan, etc.
I can't go/meet someone ..., etc.

Unit 3, Exercise 14

Student B

You are a building contractor. Your estimate for additional rooms in the hotel is as follows:
For each new double/twin room up to four new rooms, £40,000 each. For each additional double/twin room above four, £25,000 each.
For a ground floor suite without terrace £80,000. For the terrace, add £20,000 to this figure.
For a conference room on its own, £80,000.
For an exhibition room on its own, £80,000.
For a conference room linked to an adjoining exhibition room, £130,000.

Unit 4, Exercise 13

You are the hotel Maintenance Engineer. Here is the information needed to answer Student A:

— You are very busy just at this moment, but you will examine the TV set if Student A gets a porter to carry it to your Workshop.

— You do not deal with telephones yourself. Student A should contact the Switchboard Operator, who will contact the telephone company.
— You will come and look at the leaking water pipe sometime in the next hour.
— Student A should try to get help from a housekeeper or a porter to shut the window. However, you will help if necessary when you come to look at the leaking pipe in Room 119.
— Student A should be able to replace the bulb herself. She will find a bulb on a shelf of the store on Floor 2.

Unit 5, Exercise 10

Student B

You are the Reception Clerk at the Cliff Hotel. Here are the rates:

Rate Tariff

Effective September 1988/1989

All rates per person
bed and breakfast, per night £11.00, per week £65.00
set lunch £5.00
set dinner £7.00
bar meals and a la carte meals also available

half board, including dinner   per week £100.00
full board, all meals   per week £130.00

Special weekend rate, all meals
Friday Dinner – Sunday lunch   £40.00

Special midweek rate, all meals
Tuesday Dinner – Sunday lunch   £37.50

The hotel has full central heating and a comfortable residents' lounge; it is licensed to serve alcohol. There are excellent walks from the hotel along the shore in either direction. There is a dinner-dance at weekends, and a band in the bar most nights to lead residents in a sing-song.

Unit 6, Exercise 14

Student B

You are a reservations clerk in a hotel. Rooms are available as follows:

Tonight and tomorrow night you have only a double room with toilet but without bathroom, rate £41 per night, or an extra-large 'family' room with four beds at £55 per night. This room has a bathroom en suite.

For the remaining nights of this week you will have double rooms with and without bathroom available. You can put an extra bed into any double room to accommodate a child. There is no extra charge for children under twelve. The usual rate for a double room with bathroom is £46 a night.

Business in the hotel has been poor this year, and the Manager has allowed you some flexibility in the rates you charge, especially in cases where guests have to change rooms during their stay.

Unit 9, Exercise 13

Student B

You have arrived at the hotel with your wife (or with your husband). You are extremely tired, as you have arrived in the country after a 14-hour flight, then driven a car for five hours. All you want to do is to find a room — quickly — have a nice hot bath, and go to sleep. Try to book a suitable room from the Receptionist.

Student C

You are the Housekeeper. Sometimes you have a better idea of guests' intentions than the Receptionist does. Mr/s Stevens in Room 101 (T) have just told you that they are going to check out this morning. On the other hand, Mr/s Wells in Room 104 (TB) have just told you that they would like to stay on for one more night, and not leave this morning as they had planned. You don't know the intentions of Mr Barclay in room 102 (S). As far as you know, Mr/s Rogers are staying on in Room 103 (D), but you have said goodbye to Mr Reid from Room 105 (SB). You have just looked into Room 106 (DB), which has been freshly painted. The paint is dry now, but you are keeping the windows open in order to keep the room well-ventilated.

Unit 10, Exercise 14

Student B

You are the Switchboard Operator at the Paradise Hotel. The time now is 14.30. You take the call from Student A (on a very bad line) and after some difficulty put him through to the Assistant Manager (Student C). Several urgent calls come in for C while A and C are talking. You interrupt the conversation several times to ask C if he wants to take the calls. (You can use sentences like 'I've got Mr Fabrizzi on the line from Rome. He says it's very important ..., etc.')

Student C

You are the Assistant Manager at the Paradise Hotel. The time is 14.30. A call comes through for you, but the line is bad, so you constantly have to ask the caller to repeat the information. From time to time the Switchboard Operator interrupts your conversation to ask you if you want to take other calls — but you do not think these calls are very important.

You are busy every day of the week this week, except for tomorrow afternoon, or from nine to ten in the morning of the day after tomorrow — but this is the time when you go to your weekly keep-fit class, and you do not want to miss the class unless there is a very good reason.

~~ TONIGHT! TONIGHT! ~~

Magic and mystery from David Diabolo – magician extraordinaire

Songs old and new from Lana Shirene
Great entertainment for all the family!
East Reception Room – 19.00-21.00

Sooty and the Cat
A film for younger guests
Hotel TV network 16.30-18.30

Manita and her dancers
Great cabaret act – adults only
Indigo Room – 22.30-00.30

!!Bingo!!
Lottery game with fabulous prizes!
Fireside Lounge – 20.00-21.30

~~ TONIGHT! TONIGHT! ~~

EAT IN STYLE AT THE GRAND HOTEL!

For the finest in French/Italian haute cuisine
try our **Gourmet Restaurant** (top floor)
open 19.00-23.30.
Advance booking recommended.

The Huntsman's Grill
Hotel ground floor – the best steak-house in town.
Man-sized meals at moderate prices.
(No reservation necessary for hotel guests).

FLIGHTS

The Travel Agency on the first floor will make flight reservations and confirmations for all airlines except Mango Airlines. Passengers travelling by Mango Airways should contact the Mango Airways Office in the city (11 Independence Street, telephone 655031).

LOST PROPERTY

Items found in the hotel are sent to our Lost Property Office which is administered by the Hall Porter's Department. Contact the Hall Porter for information (telephone 5). For any item recently left in a room the Chief Housekeeper may be able to help (telephone 7).

TENNIS

There is a tennis court in the Sports Complex (behind the hotel, tel.03). Guests wishing to play on this court are advised to book early in the day, as it is extremely popular.

The Grand Hotel has negotiated special terms for guests wishing to use facilities in the Corniche Tennis Club (on the Corniche, about 1 km from the hotel). Guests can obtain temporary membership at a reduced cost. For details, contact the club secretary, Corniche Tennis Club, tel. 442091.

Unit 11, Exercise 13

Student B

You stayed at the Viceroy Hotel. When you phoned Room Service there was never any reply. The TV set in your room wasn't working. There was a good, inexpensive restaurant in the basement of the hotel. The hotel was not on the main road and there was no problem about parking. When you left a shirt to be washed it took two days to get it back. There was no photocopier for public use, but the Receptionist made copies of any papers you needed and you did not have to pay anything.

(You can add two or three extra services and/or problems if you wish.)

Unit 12, Exercise 14

Student B

You are an enquiries clerk in the hotel. The information in the posters and cards below will help you to answer guests' enquiries, but it may not be necessary to tell the guest everything. Find out what the guest wants and give information accordingly.

Unit 14, Exercise 16

Student B

You are making some complaints about your bill to the Assistant Manager (Student A), because:

— You think you have been charged for a telephone call that you did not make.
— You have been charged for an 'English breakfast' instead of a 'continental breakfast'.
— You have been charged for 'laundry', although the laundry lost some items of clothing.
— You have been charged for 'dinner' last night although you were dissatisfied with the food and complained about your meal at the time.
— A service charge of 10 per cent has been added to the bill, although you were not informed about this extra charge, and you feel the service does not deserve it.

Tell the Assistant Manager what you think, and find out what he is going to do about it.

Unit 15, Exercise 16

Student B

You are the Hotel Manager. As politely as possible, try to make Student A aware of the following facts;

— If a flight arrives late, it is not the responsibility of the hotel.
— If guests do not check in before 21.00, and do not inform the hotel it is quite normal for the hotel to let the room to another guest.
— If the guest finds a room unsatisfactory, the management will do its best to provide a more suitable room, if there are vacant rooms.
— The guest had in fact asked for a wake-up call for 06.30 on checking in the previous night, unless a 'Do not disturb' card is hung on the door handle.
— It is normal for the chambermaid to come in around 9.30.

Unit 16, Exercise 15

Student B

You are organizing a conference on behalf of the International Salesmen's Federation. The details of the conference are as follows:

Duration of conference: 4 days
Number of participants: 120
Types of meetings include:
— Lectures to all participants
— Division into eight groups for seminars and workshops
— Video presentations by senior salesmen to demonstrate selling techniques.
— Role-play of selling situations, to be viewed on closed circuit TV and recorded on video.
Secretarial support required:
— One full-time secretary during the conference
— Full copying and typing services for production of handouts and photocopies.
Other facilities:
— Refreshment facilities (coffee, snacks and bar facilities).

You are willing to pay up to $1200 a day for use of the conference premises. For this price you would expect various facilities to be included, as follows:
— Use of TV equipment, secretarial assistance, use of the photocopier, and coffee during morning and afternoon breaks.
You would not expect this price to include:
— Food, alcoholic or soft drinks
— Copies of handouts amounting to more than 1000 pages per day.

As part of the complete package, you would hope to have all participants staying in the hotel, with a favourable reduction on normal rack rates.

Talk to the Manager of the Great Ship Hotel. Find out what he can offer you. Try to negotiate a suitable rate.

International telephone dialling service

You can dial overseas numbers directly from your room.
For overseas person-to-person calls and reverse charge (collect) calls, please call the operator by dialling 9.
When calling overseas directly, please wait approximately 30 seconds to be connected to your party after you finish dialling. Please dial the following.

Long Distance Key Code 0	→	Int'l Dialling Code 00	→	Country Code	→	Area Code	→	Local Telephone Number

Service Area	Country Code

THE AMERICAS

Alaska	1
Argentina	54
Aruba	297
Bolivia	591
Brazil	55
Canada	1
Chile	56
Colombia	57
Costa Rica	506
Ecuador	593
El Salvador	503
Guatemala	502
Guyana	592
Honduras	504
Mexico	52
Netherlands Antilles	599
Nicaragua	505
Panama	507
Paraguay	595
Surinam (Rep. of)	597
USA	1
Uruguay	598
Venezuela	58

ASIA

Bahrain	973
Brunei	673
Burma	95
Cyprus	357
Hong Kong	852
India	91
Indonesia	62
Iran	98
Iraq	964
Israel	972
Jordan	962
Korea (Rep. of)	82
Kuwait	965
Macao	853
Malaysia	60
Maldives	960
Oman	968
Pakistan	92

Service Area	Country Code

Philippines	63	**OCEANIA**	
Qatar	974	American Samoa	684
Saudi Arabia	966	Australia	61
Singapore	65	Fiji	679
Sri Lanka	94	Guam	671
Syria	963	Hawaii	1
Taiwan	886	Marshall Is.	692
Thailand	66	Micronesia	691
United Arab Emirates	971	Nauru	674
Yemen Arab Rep.	967	New Caledonia	687
		New Zealand	64
EUROPE		Papua New Guinea	675
Andorra	34	Saipan Is.	670
Austria	43	Solomon Is.	677
Azores Is.	351	Tonga	676
Belgium	32	Vanuatu	678
Czechoslovakia	42	Western Samoa	685
Denmark	45		
Faroe Is.	298		
Finland	358		
France	33	**AFRICA**	
Germany (Demo. Rep.)	37	Algeria	213
Germany (Fed. Rep. of)	49	Angola	244
Gibraltar	350	Canary Is.	34
Greece	30	Egypt	20
Hungary	36	Gabon	241
Iceland	354	Ivory Coast	225
Ireland	353	Kenya	254
Italy	39	Lesotho	266
Lichtenstein	41	Madagascar	261
Luxembourg	352	Madeira	351
Malta	356	Malawi	265
Monaco	33	Mauritius	230
Netherlands	31	Namibia	264
Norway	47	Morocco	212
Poland	48	Mozambique	258
Portugal	351	Niger	227
Romania	40	Nigeria	234
San Marino	39	Senegal	221
Spain	34	Seychelles (Rep. of)	248
Sweden	46	South Africa	27
Switzerland	41	Spanish North Africa	34
Turkey	90	Swaziland	268
United Kingdom	44	Tanzania	255
USSR	7	Tunisia	216
Vatican	39	Uganda	256
Yugoslavia	38	Zambia	260